Justification
by
Faith Alone

"But to him that worketh not, but believeth on
Him that justifieth the ungodly, his faith
is counted for righteousness."
Romans 4:5

by

Jonathan Edwards

Edited by Dr. Don Kistler

Soli Deo Gloria Publications
. . . for instruction in righteousness . . .

Soli Deo Gloria Publications
P.O. Box 451, Morgan, PA 15064
(412) 221-1901/FAX 221-1902
www.SDGbooks.com

*

Justification by Faith Alone was retypeset from the 1838
Hickman edition of *The Works of Jonathan Edwards.*
This Soli Deo Gloria edition, in which spelling,
grammar, and formatting changes have
been made, is © 2000 by Soli Deo Gloria.

*

ISBN 1-57358-107-0

*

2nd printing — 2002

Contents

Publisher's Preface

This book was originally the substance of two public lectures delivered by this great preacher in Northampton, Massachusetts, in November 1734. It was one of his earliest printed sermons, published in 1738 as part of his *Discourses on Various Important Subjects*.

The material in those two lectures was expanded for publication, and takes up more than 30 pages of tiny, two-column print in the Hickman edition of Edwards's *Works,* and close to 160 in this present format. Not even a well-heeled Puritan congregation could have endured a sermon of that length in one setting!

According to Dr. Samuel Logan, in the *Westminster Theological Journal* (Volume XLVI, Spring 1984, pp. 26–52), Edwards was endeavoring to respond to an encroaching Arminianism in Northampton, as well as an abiding antinomianism in the colonies since the days of Anne Hutchinson. And Jonathan Edwards is nothing if not thorough in his treatment of any subject he might address.

When Soli Deo Gloria published a paperback compilation on the same theme some years ago, it had been our original intent to include these lectures as a chapter. The late Dr. John H. Gerstner, a contributing author to that book, said that if we were going to use Edwards's sermon on justification by faith alone, no further material would be necessary! We trust that having both titles in print will redound even more to God's glory!

Soli Deo Gloria!

Chapter 1

The Introduction to the Doctrine

"But to him that worketh not, but believeth on Him
that justifieth the ungodly, his faith is counted
for righteousness." Romans 4:5

The following things may be noted in this verse:
1. Justification respects a man as ungodly. This is evident by the words "that justifieth the ungodly," which cannot imply less than that God, in the act of justification, has no regard for anything in the person justified, such as godliness or any goodness in him, but that immediately before this act God sees him only as an ungodly creature. So that godliness in the person to be justified is not so antecedent to his justification as to be the ground of it. When it is said that God justifies the ungodly, it is absurd to suppose that our godliness, taken as some goodness in us, is the ground of our justification. We might as well suppose, when it says that Christ gave sight to the blind, that sight was prior to and the ground of that act of mercy in Christ; or, if it is said that such a one by his bounty has made a poor man rich, we might as well suppose that the wealth of this poor man was the ground of this bounty towards him, and was the price by which it was procured.
2. It appears that by "him that worketh not" in this verse is not meant one who merely does not conform to the ceremonial law, because "them that worketh not" and "the ungodly" are evidently synonymous expres-

1

sions, as appears by the manner of their connection. If not, then to what purpose is the latter expression, "the ungodly," brought in? The context gives no other occasion for it but to show that, by the grace of the gospel, God in justification has no regard to any godliness of ours. The previous verse says, "Now to him that worketh is the reward not reckoned of grace, but of debt." In that verse, it is evident that gospel grace consists in the reward being given without works; and in this verse, which immediately follows it, and in a sense is connected with it, gospel grace consists in a man's being justified while ungodly. By this it is most plain that by "him that worketh not" and "him that is ungodly" are meant the same thing. Therefore, not only works of the ceremonial law are excluded in this business of justification, but works of morality and godliness.

3. It is evident in these words that by the faith here spoken of, by which we are justified, is not meant the same thing as a course of obedience or righteousness, since the expression by which this faith is here denoted is "believing on Him that justifieth the ungodly." They who oppose the "Solifidians," as they call them, greatly insist that we should take the words of Scripture concerning this doctrine in their most natural and obvious meaning. And how they cry out against our clouding this doctrine with obscure metaphors and unintelligible figures of speech! But is this to interpret Scripture according to its most obvious meaning, when the Scripture speaks of our "believing on Him that justifieth the ungodly," or the readers of His law, to say that the meaning of it is performing a course of obedience to His law and avoiding the breaches of it? Believing on God as a justifier certainly is a different thing from

submitting to God as a Lawgiver; especially believing on Him as a justifier of the ungodly, or rebels against the Lawgiver.

4. It is evident that the subject of justification is looked upon as destitute of any righteousness in himself, by that expression that his faith is counted, or imputed to him for righteousness. The phrase, as the apostle uses it here and in the context, manifestly imports that God, in His sovereign grace, is pleased, in His dealings with the sinner, so to regard one who has no righteousness that the consequence shall be the same as if he had. This, however, may be from the respect it bears to some thing that is indeed righteous. It is plain that this is the force of the expression in the preceding verses.

In the next-to-the-last verse, it is manifest that the apostle lays the stress of his argument for the free grace of God—from the text of the Old Testament about Abraham—on the word "counted" or "imputed"; and this is the thing that he supposed God to show His grace in: in this counting something for righteousness in His consequential dealings with Abraham that was no righteousness in itself. And in the verse which immediately precedes the text ("Now to him that worketh is the reward not reckoned of grace, but of debt"), the word there translated "reckoned" is the same that in the other verses is rendered "imputed" and "counted." It is as much as if the apostle had said, "As for him who works, there is no need of any gracious reckoning or counting it for righteousness, and causing the reward to follow as if it were a righteousness; for if he has works, he has that which is a righteousness in itself, to which the reward properly belongs."

This is further evident by the words that follow in verse 6: "Even as David also described the blessedness of the man unto whom God imputeth righteousness without works." What can here be meant by "imputing righteousness without works" but imputing righteousness to him who has none of his own? Verses 7–8: "Saying, 'Blessed are they whose iniquities are forgiven, and whose sins are covered: blessed is the man to whom the Lord will not impute sin.' " How do these words of David suit the apostle's purpose? Or how do they prove that righteousness is imputed without works unless it is because the word "imputed" is used, and the subject of the imputation is mentioned as a sinner, and consequently destitute of a moral righteousness? For David says no such thing as that he is forgiven without the works of the ceremonial law; there is no hint of the ceremonial law or reference to it, in the words. I will therefore venture to infer this doctrine from these words for the subject of my present discourse.

DOCTRINE. We are justified only by faith in Christ, not by any manner of virtue or goodness of our own.

Such an assertion as this, I am aware, many would be ready to call absurd, as betraying a great deal of ignorance, and containing much inconsistency; but I desire everyone's patience till I have done. I hope to:

• Explain the meaning of it, and show how I would be understood by such an assertion.

• Proceed to the consideration of the evidence of the truth of it.

• Show how evangelical obedience is concerned in this affair.

• Answer objections.

• Consider the importance of the doctrine.

Chapter 2

The Meaning of the Doctrine

I would now explain the meaning of the doctrine, or show in what sense I assert it, and endeavor to evidence the truth of it. This may be done in answer to these two questions:

First, what is meant by being justified?

Second, what is meant when it is said that this is by faith alone, without any manner of virtue or goodness of our own?

1. What is meant in Scripture by being justified?

A person is said to be justified when he is approved by God as free from the guilt of sin and its deserved punishment, and as having that righteousness belonging to him that entitles him to the reward of life. That we should take the word in such a sense—and understand it as the judge's accepting a person as having both a negative and positive righteousness belonging to him, and looking on him therefore not only as free from any obligation to punishment, but also as just and righteous, and so entitled to a positive reward—is not only most agreeable to the etymology and natural import of the word (which signifies "to pass one for righteous in judgment") but also manifestly agreeable to the force of the word as used in Scripture.

Some suppose that nothing more is intended in Scripture by "justification" than the mere remission of sins. If so, it is very strange if we consider the nature of the case; for it is most evident, and none will deny it, that it is with respect to the rule or law of God we are under that we are said in Scripture to be either justified or condemned. Now what is it to justify a person as the subject of a law or rule but to judge him as standing right with respect to that rule? To justify a person in a particular case is to approve of him as standing right, as subject to the law in that case; and to justify in general is to pass judgment on him as standing right in a state correspondent to the law or rule in general. But certainly, in order for a person to be looked on as standing right with respect to the rule in general, or in a state corresponding with the law of God, more is needful than not having the guilt of sin; for whatever that law is, whether it is a new or an old one, doubtless something positive is needed in order for it to be answered.

We are no more justified by the voice of the law, or the voice of him who judges according to it, by a mere pardon of sin than Adam, our first surety, was justified by the law at the first point of his existence, before he had fulfilled the obedience of the law or had so much as any trial whether he would fulfill it or not. If Adam had finished his course of perfect obedience, he would have been justified. And certainly his justification would have implied something more than what is merely negative; he would have been approved of as having fulfilled the righteousness of the law, and accordingly would have been entitled to the reward of it. So Christ, our second Surety (in whose justification all whose Surety He is are virtually justified), was not justified till He had done the work the Father had appointed for Him, and kept the Father's commandments through all trials—and then, in His resurrection, He was justified. When He had been put to death in the flesh, but quickened by the Spirit (1 Peter 3:18), then He who was manifest in the flesh was justified in the Spirit (1 Timothy 3:16); but when God justified Christ in raising Him from the dead, He not only released Him from His humiliation for sin, and acquitted Him from any further suffering or abasement for it, but admitted Him to that eternal and immortal life, and to the beginning of that exaltation that was the reward for what He had done.

And, indeed, the justification of a believer is no other than his being admitted to communion in the justification of this Head and Surety of all believers; for as Christ suffered the punishment of sin (not as a private person, but as our Surety), so when after this suffering He was raised from the dead, He was therein justified—not as a private person, but as the Surety and representative of all who would believe in Him. So that He was raised again not only for His own justification, but also for ours, according to the apostle in Romans 4:25: "Who was delivered for our offenses, and raised again for our justification." And therefore it is that the apostle says, as he does in Romans 8:34: "Who is he that condemneth? It is Christ that died, yea rather, that is risen again."

But that a believer's justification implies not only remission of sins, or acquittal from the wrath due to it, but also an admittance to a title to that glory which is the reward of righteousness, is more directly taught in the Scripture, particularly in Romans 5:1–2, where the apostle mentions both of these as joint benefits implied in justification: "Therefore being justified by faith, we have peace with God through our Lord Jesus

Christ, by whom also we have access into this grace
wherein we stand, and rejoice in hope of the glory of
God." So remission of sin, and an inheritance among
those who are sanctified are mentioned together as
jointly obtained by faith in Christ. Acts 26:18: "That they
may receive forgiveness of sins, and inheritance among
them that are sanctified through faith that is in Me."
Both of these are doubtless implied in that passing
from death to life of which Christ speaks as the fruit of
faith, and which He opposes to condemnation. John
5:24: "Verily I say unto you, he that heareth My word,
and believeth on Him that sent Me, hath everlasting
life, and shall not come into condemnation, but is
passed from death unto life."

2. I proceed now to show what is meant when it is
said that this justification is by faith only, and not by
any virtue or goodness of our own.

This inquiry may be divided into two parts: how it is
by faith, and how it is by faith alone, without any manner of goodness of ours.

How Justification Is by Faith

Here the great difficulty has been about the import
and force of the particle "by," or what is that influence
that faith has in the affair of justification that is expressed in Scripture by being justified by faith.

Here, if I may humbly express what seems evident to
me, though faith is indeed the condition of justification, so that nothing else is, yet this matter is not
clearly and sufficiently explained by saying that faith is
the condition of justification; that is because the word
seems ambiguous, both in common use and also as

used in divinity. In one sense, Christ alone performs
the condition of our justification and salvation; in still
another sense faith is the condition of justification; in
another sense other qualifications and acts are conditions of salvation and justification too. There seems to
be a great deal of ambiguity in such expressions as are
commonly used (which yet we are forced to use), such
as "condition of salvation," what is required in order to
receive salvation or justification, the terms of the
covenant, and the like. I believe they are understood in
very different senses by different persons.

And besides, as the word "condition" is very often
understood in the common use of language, faith is
not the thing in us that is the condition of justification; for by the word "condition," as it is very often (and
perhaps most commonly) used, we mean anything that
may have the place of a condition in a conditional
proposition, and as such is truly connected with the
consequent, especially if the proposition holds both in
the affirmative and negative, as the condition is either
affirmed or denied. If it is that with which, or which being supposed, a thing shall be, and without which, or it
being denied, a thing shall not be, we in such a case
call it a condition of that thing. But in this sense faith
is not the only condition of salvation or justification;
for there are many things that accompany and flow
from faith, with which justification shall be, and without which it will not be, and which therefore are found
to be put in Scripture in conditional propositions with
justification and salvation, in multitudes of places.
These include love to God, love to our brethren, forgiving men their trespasses, and many other good qualifications and acts. And there are many other things be-

sides faith which are directly proposed to us to be pursued or performed by us in order to obtain eternal life, which if they are done or obtained, we shall have eternal life; if they are not done or not obtained, we shall surely perish. To say that faith is the only condition of justification in that sense would not express the sense of that phrase of Scripture of being justified by faith.

There is a difference between being justified by a thing, and that thing universally, necessarily, and inseparably attending justification; for the latter criterion is also met by a great many things that we are not said to be justified by. It is not the inseparable connection with justification that the Holy Ghost would signify (or that is naturally signified) by such a phrase, but some particular influence that faith has in the affair, or some certain dependence that effect has on its influence.

Some, aware of this, have supposed that the influence or dependence might well be expressed by faith's being the instrument of our justification; but this concept has been misunderstood and injuriously represented, and ridiculed by those who deny the doctrine of justification by faith alone, supposing that faith is used as an instrument in the hand of God whereby He performed and brought to pass that act of His, that is, approving and justifying the believer. Whereas it was not intended that faith was the instrument wherewith God justifies, but the instrument wherewith we receive justification; not the instrument wherewith the Justifier acts in justifying, but wherewith the receiver of justification acts in accepting justification.

Yet it must be acknowledged that this is an obscure way of speaking, and there must certainly be some impropriety in calling faith an instrument wherewith we receive or accept justification; for the very persons who thus explain the matter speak of faith as being the reception or acceptance itself. And if this is so, how can it be the *instrument* of reception or acceptance? Certainly there is a difference between the act and the instrument. Besides, by their own descriptions of faith, Christ, the Mediator by whom and by whose righteousness we are justified, is more directly the object of this acceptance and justification, which is the benefit arising therefrom more indirectly. And therefore, if faith is an instrument, it is more properly the instrument by which we receive Christ than the instrument by which we receive justification.

But I humbly conceive that we have been ready to look too far to find out what that influence of faith in our justification is, or what is that dependence of this effect on faith, signified by the expression of "being justified by faith," all the while overlooking that which is most obviously pointed forth in the expression: that (there being a Mediator who has purchased justification) faith in this Mediator is that which renders it a fit and suitable thing in the sight of God that the believer, rather than others, should have this purchased benefit assigned to him. God sees it to be more fit and suitable that this thing should be assigned to some rather than others because He sees them as differently qualified; that qualification wherein the fitness for this benefit, as the case stands, consists is that thing in us by which we are justified. If Christ had not come into the world and died to purchase justification, no qualification whatsoever in us could render it a meet or fit thing that we should be justified. But the case being as it now stands, that Christ has actually purchased justification by His own blood for infinitely unworthy creatures, there may be certain qualification found in some persons, which, either from the relation it bears to the Mediator and His merits or on some other account, is the thing that in the sight of God renders it a proper and decent thing that they should have an interest in this purchased benefit, and the lack of which renders an unfit and unsuitable thing that they should have it.

The wisdom of God in His constitutions doubtless appears much in the fitness and beauty of them, so that those things are established to be done that are fit to be done, and that those things are connected in His constitution that are agreeable to another. So God justifies a believer according to His revealed constitution, without doubt, because He sees something in this qualification that, as the case stands, renders it a fit thing that such a person should be justified—whether it is because faith is the instrument, or, as it were, the hand by which He who has purchased justification is apprehended and accepted, or because it is the acceptance itself, or whatever else. To be justified is to be approved by God as a proper subject of pardon, with a right to eternal life; and therefore, when it is said that we are justified by faith, what else can be understood by it than that faith is that by which we are rendered approvable, fitly so, and indeed, as the case stands, proper subjects of this benefit?

This is something different from faith being the condition of justification, though inseparably connected with justification. So are many other things besides faith; and yet nothing in us *but* faith renders it fitting that we should have justification assigned to us. This I shall now show.

How Justification Is by Faith Alone

This may seem to some to be attended with two difficulties. First, how can justification be said to be by faith alone without any virtue or goodness of ours, when faith itself is a virtue and one part of our goodness, and is not only some manner of goodness of ours, but is a very excellent qualification, and one chief part of the inherent holiness of a Christian? And if it is a part of our inherent goodness or excellence (whether it is this part or any other) that renders it a decent or congruous thing that we should have this benefit of Christ assigned to us, how is this less than what they mean who talk of a merit of congruity? Second, if this part of our Christian holiness qualifies us in the sight of God for this benefit of Christ, and renders it a fit or meet thing in His sight that we should have it, why should not other parts of holiness and conformity to God, which are also very excellent, and have as much of the image of Christ in them, and are no less lovely in God's eyes, qualify us as much, and have as much influence to render us meet, in God's sight, for such a benefit as this? Therefore I answer:

When it is said that we are not justified by any righteousness or goodness of our own, what is meant is that it is not out of respect to the excellence or goodness of any qualifications or acts in us whatsoever that God judges it proper that this benefit of Christ should be ours; and it is not in any way on account of any excellence or value present in faith that it appears in the sight of God as a proper thing that he who believes should have this benefit of Christ assigned to him, but purely from the relation faith has to the person in

whom this benefit is to be had, or as it unites to that
Mediator in and by whom we are justified. Here, for
greater clarity, I would particularly explain myself under several propositions.

(1) It is certain that there is some union or relation that the people of Christ stand in to Him. This re-
lationship is expressed in Scripture, from time to time,
by "being in Christ," and is represented frequently by
those metaphors of being "members of Christ," or being united to Him as members are to the Head, or as
branches to the stock. It is compared to a marriage
union between husband and wife. I do not now pretend
to determine of what sort this union is; nor is it necessary to my present purpose to enter into any manner of
disputes about it. If any are disgusted at the word
"union," as being obscure and unintelligible, the word
"relation" equally serves my purpose. I do not now desire to determine any more about it than all, of all sorts,
will readily allow, that is, that there is a peculiar relation between true Christians and Christ which there is
not between Him and others. And this is signified by
those metaphoric expressions in Scripture of "being in
Christ" or being "members of Christ."

(2) This relation or union to Christ whereby
Christians are said to be "in Christ" (whatever it is) is
the ground of their right to His benefits. This needs no
proof; the reason of the thing at first glance demon-
strates it. It is exceedingly evident also from Scripture.
1 John 5:12: "He that hath the Son hath life; and he that
hath not the Son hath not life." 1 Corinthians 1:30: "Of
Him are ye in Christ Jesus, who of God is made unto us
righteousness." First we must be "in Him," and then He
will be made righteousness or justification to us.

Ephesians 1:6: "Who hath made us accepted in the Beloved." Being in Him is the ground of our being accepted.

So it is in those unions to which the Holy Ghost has thought fit to compare this one. The union of the members of the body with the head is the ground of their partaking of the life of the head; it is the union of the branches to the stock which is the ground of their partaking of the sap and life of the stock; it is the relation of the wife to the husband that is the ground of her joint interest in his estate; they are looked upon, in several respects, as one in law. So there is a legal union between Christ and true Christians, so that (as all except Socinians allow) one, in some respects, is accepted for the other by the Supreme Judge.

(3) And thus it is that faith is the qualification in any person that renders it meet in the sight of God that he should be looked upon as having Christ's satisfaction and righteousness belonging to him, that is, because it is that in him which, on his part, makes up this union between him and Christ. By what has been just now observed, it is a person's being, to use the Scripture phrase, "in Christ" that is the ground of having His satisfaction and merits belong to him, and a right to the benefits procured thereby. The reason for it is plain; it is easy to see how our having Christ's merits and benefits belonging to us follows from our having (if I may so speak) Christ Himself belonging to us, or our being united to Him. And if so, it must also be easy to see how, or in what manner, that in a person which on his part makes up the union between his soul and Christ should be the thing on account of which God looks on it as meet that he should have Christ's merits

belonging to him. It is a very different thing for God to
assign to a particular person a right to Christ's merits
and benefits out of regard for a qualification in him in
this respect—that is, His doing it for him out of respect
for the value or loveliness of that qualification—rather
than as a reward of its excellency.

As there is nobody but will allow that there is a peculiar relation between Christ and His true disciples, by
which they are in some sense in Scripture said to be
one, so I suppose there is nobody but will allow that
there may be something that the true Christian does on
his part whereby he is active in coming into this relation or union, some uniting act, or that which is done
towards this union or relation (or whatever any is
pleased to call it) on the Christian's part. Now faith I
suppose to be this act.

I do not now pretend to define justifying faith, or to
determine precisely how much is contained in it, but
only to determine this much concerning it: justifying
faith is that by which the soul, which before was separated and alienated from Christ, unites itself to Him, or
ceases to be any longer in that state of alienation, and
comes into that aforementioned union or relation to
Him. Or, to use the Scripture phrase, it is that by which
the soul comes to Christ and receives Him. This is evident by the Scripture's use of these very expressions to
signify faith. John 6:35–40: "He that cometh to Me shall
never hunger; and he that believeth on Me shall never
thirst. But I said unto you that ye also have seen Me and
believe not. All that the Father giveth Me shall come to
Me; and him that cometh to Me I will in no wise cast
out, for I came down from heaven not to do Mine own
will, but the will of Him that sent Me. And this is the

will of Him that sent Me, that everyone which seeth the Son and believeth on Him may have everlasting life; and I will raise him up at the last day." John 5:38–40: "Whom He hath sent, Him ye believe not. Search the Scriptures, for they testify of Me. And ye will not come unto Me that ye might have life." Verses 43–44: "I am come in My Father's name, and ye receive Me not; if another shall come in his own name, him ye will receive. How can ye believe, which receive honor one of another?" John 1:12: "But as many as received Him, to them gave He power to become the sons of God, even to them that believe on His name."

If it is said that these are obscure figures of speech, which, however well they might be understood of old by those who commonly used such metaphors, are with difficulty understood now, I allow that the expressions of receiving Christ and coming to Christ are metaphoric expressions; and if I should allow them to be obscure metaphors, yet this much at least is certainly plain in them: faith is that by which those who before were separated and at a distance from Christ (that is to say, were not so related and united to Him as His people are) cease to be any longer at such a distance, and come into that relation and nearness—unless they are so unintelligible that nothing at all can be understood by them.

God does not give those who believe a union with or an interest in the Savior as a reward for faith, but only because faith is the soul's active uniting with Christ, or is itself the very act of union on their part. God sees it as fitting that, in order for a union to be established between two intelligent active beings or persons, so that they should be looked upon as one, there should be the mutual act of both, that each should receive the other, as actively joining themselves one to another. God, in requiring this in order for us to be united with Christ as one of His people, treats men as reasonable creatures, capable of acting and choosing, and hence sees it fit that they alone who are one with Christ by their own action should be looked upon as one in law. What is real in the union between Christ and His people is the foundation of what is legal; that is, it is something really in them and between them, uniting them. That is the ground of the suitableness of their being accounted as one by the Judge. And if there is any act or qualification in believers which is of that uniting nature—that makes it meet on that account that the Judge should look upon them and accept them as one—no wonder that on account of the same act or qualification He should accept the satisfaction and merits of the one for the other, as if these were their own satisfaction and merits. This necessarily follows, or rather is implied.

And thus it is that faith justifies, or gives an interest in Christ's satisfaction and merits and a right to the benefits procured thereby, since it thus makes Christ and the believer one in the acceptance of the Supreme Judge. It is by faith that we have a title to eternal life because it is by faith that we have the Son of God by whom life is. The Apostle John (in these words from 1 John 5:12: "He that hath the Son hath life") seems evidently to have respect to those words of Christ of which he gives an account in his gospel, in John 3:36: "He that believeth on the Son hath everlasting life; and he that believeth not the Son shall not see life." And where the Scripture speaks of faith as the soul's receiving or coming to Christ, it also speaks of this receiving, coming to, or joining with Christ as the ground of an interest in His benefits. "But as many as received Him, to them gave He power" to become the sons of God. "Ye will not come unto Me that ye might have life." And there is a wide difference between its being suitable that Christ's satisfaction and merits should be theirs who believe, because an interest in that satisfaction and merit is a fit reward of faith, or a suitable testimony of God's respect to the amiableness and excellence of that grace and its being suitable that Christ's satisfaction and merits should be theirs because Christ and they are so united that in the eyes of the Judge they may be looked upon and taken as one.

Although, on account of faith in the believer, it is in the sight of God fit and congruous that he who believes should be looked upon both as in Christ and also as having an interest in His merits in the way that has now been explained, yet it appears that this is very different from a merit of congruity, or indeed any moral congruity at all.

There are two types of fitness in a desirable state. I do not know how to give them distinguishing names other than to call the one a *moral* and the other a *natural* fitness. A person has a moral fitness for a state when his moral excellence commends him to it, or when his being put into such a good state is but a suitable testimony of regard to the moral excellence, value, or amiableness of any of his qualifications or acts. A person has a natural fitness for a state when it appears meet and decent that he should be in such a state or circumstances only from the natural concord or agreeableness there is between such qualifications and such circumstances; not because the qualifications are lovely or unlovely, but only because the qualifications and the circumstances are like one another, or in their nature are suitable and agree or unite one to another. And it is on this latter account alone that God looks on it as fitting (by a natural fitness) that he whose heart sincerely unites itself to Christ as his Savior should be looked upon as united to that Savior, and so to have an interest in Him, and not from any moral fitness between the excellence of such a qualification as faith and such a glorious blessedness as having an interest in Christ. God's bestowing Christ and His benefits on a soul in consequence of faith, out of regard only to the natural concord there is between such a qualification of a soul and such a union with Christ and interest in Him, makes the case widely differ from what it would be if He bestowed this out of regard to any moral suitableness. For, in the former case, it is only from God's love of order that He bestows these things on account of faith. In the latter, God does it out of love for the grace of faith itself. God will neither look to Christ's merit as ours, nor grant His benefits to us till we are in Christ; nor will He look upon us as being in Him without an active union of our hearts and souls to Him, because He is a wise being and delights in order, and not in confusion, and that things should be together or asunder according to their nature.

God's making such a constitution is a testimony of His love of order. If it were out of regard to any moral fitness or suitableness between faith and such blessedness, it would be a testimony of His love for the act or qualification itself. The one supposes this divine constitution to be a manifestation of God's regard for the beauty of the act of faith; the other only supposes it to be a manifestation of His regard to the beauty of the order there is in uniting those things that have a natural agreement, congruity, and union one with the other. Indeed, a moral suitableness or fitness to a state includes a natural one; for if there is a moral suitableness that a person should be in such a state, there is also a natural suitableness, but such a natural suitableness as I have described by no means necessarily includes a moral one.

This is plainly what our divines intend when they say that faith does not justify as a work or a righteousness, that is, that it does not justify as a part of our moral goodness or excellence, or that it does not justify as man was to have been justified by the covenant of works, which was to have a title to eternal life given him by God in testimony of His being pleased with a man's works, or His regard for the inherent excellence and beauty of that man's obedience. And this is certainly what the Apostle Paul means when he so firmly insists that we are not justified by works, that is, that we are not justified by them as good works, or by any goodness, value, or excellence in our works.

For the proof of this I shall mention but one thing, and that is that the apostle, from time to time, speaks of our not being justified by works as the thing that excludes all boasting (Ephesians 2:9; Romans 3:27 and 4:2). Now, how would works give occasion for boasting but if they were good? What do men boast of but something they suppose is good or excellent? And on what account do they boast of anything but for the supposed excellence that is in it?

From these things we may learn in what manner faith is the only condition of justification and salvation. For though it is not the only condition (so as alone truly to have the place of a condition in an hypothetical proposition in which justification and salvation are the consequent), yet it is the condition of justification in a manner peculiar to it, and so that nothing else has a parallel influence with it—because faith includes the whole act of union with Christ as a Savior. The entire active uniting of the soul, or the whole of what is called "coming to Christ" and "receiving Him," is called "faith" in Scripture. And however other things may be no less excellent than faith, yet it is not the nature of any other graces or virtues directly to close with Christ as a Mediator any further than they enter into the constitution of justifying faith, and belong to its nature.

Thus I have explained my meaning in asserting as a doctrine of the gospel that we are justified by faith alone without any manner of goodness of our own.

Chapter 3

The Proof of the Doctrine

I now proceed to prove this doctrine, which I shall endeavor to do in the following arguments:

ARGUMENT 1. Such is our case, and the state of things, that neither faith, nor any other qualifications or action or course of actions, does or can render it suitable that a person should have an interest in the Savior, and so a title to His benefits, on account of any excellence therein, or in any other way than as something in him may unite him to the Savior. It is not suitable that God should give fallen man an interest in Christ and His merits as a testimony of His respect to anything whatsoever as a loveliness in him. This is not suitable because, until a sinner is actually justified, it is not fitting that anything in him should be accepted by God as any excellence or amiableness of his person, or that God, by any act, should in any manner or degree testify any pleasedness with him, or favor towards him, on the account of anything inherent in him. For this there are two reasons:

1. The nature of things will not allow it. And this appears from the infinite guilt that the sinner (till justified) is under, which arises from the infinite evil or heinousness of sin. But because this is what some deny, I would therefore first establish that point, and show that sin is a thing that is indeed properly of infinite heinousness, and then show the consequence that it cannot be suitable, till the sinner is actually justified,

that God should, by any act, testify pleasedness with or
acceptance of any excellence or amiableness of his person.

That the evil and demerit of sin is infinitely great is
most demonstrably evident, because what the evil or iniquity of sin consists in is the violating of an obligation, or in doing what we should not do. And therefore,
by how much the greater the obligation is that is violated, by so much the greater is the iniquity of the viola-
tion. But certainly our obligation to love or honor any
being is great in proportion to the greatness or excellence of that being, or his worthiness to be loved and
honored. We are under greater obligations to love a
more lovely being than a less lovely one; and if a being
is infinitely excellent and lovely, our obligations to love
him are therein infinitely great. The matter is so plain
that it seems needless to say much about it.

Some have argued exceedingly against the infinite
evil of sin, saying that since it is committed against an
infinite object, then it may as well be argued that there
is also an infinite value or worthiness in holiness and
love for God because that also has an infinite object.
But the analogy does not hold in the reverse. The sin of
the creature against God is ill-deserving in proportion
to the distance between God and the creature—the
greatness of the object and the meanness of the subject
aggravate it. But it is the reverse with regard to the worthiness of the respect of the creature to God. This respect is worthless (and not worthy) in proportion to the
meanness of the subject. The greater the distance between God and the creature, the less is the creature's
respect worthy of God's notice or regard. The unworthiness of sin or opposition to God rises and is great in

proportion to the dignity of the object and inferiority of the subject; but, on the contrary, the value of respect rises in proportion to the value of the subject, and that for the plain reason that the evil of disrespect is in proportion to the obligation that lies upon the subject to the object.

This obligation is most evidently increased by the excellence and superiority of the object. But, on the contrary, the worthiness of respect to a being is in proportion to the obligation that lies on him who is the object (or rather the reason he has) to regard the subject, which certainly is in proportion to the subject's value or excellence. Sin or disrespect is evil or heinous in proportion to the degree of what it denies in the object, and, as it were, takes from it its excellence and worthiness of respect. On the contrary, respect is valuable in proportion to the value of what is given to the object in that respect, which undoubtedly (other things being equal) is great in proportion to the subject's value or worthiness of regard, because the subject, in giving his respect, can give no more than himself. So far as he gives his respect, he gives himself to the object; and therefore his gift is of greater or lesser value in proportion to the value of himself.

Hence, the love, honor, and obedience of Christ towards God have infinite value because of the excellence and dignity of the person in whom these qualifications were inherent. And the reason why we needed a person of infinite dignity to obey for us was because of our infinite meanness who had disobeyed, whereby our disobedience was infinitely aggravated. We needed someone, the worthiness of whose obedience might be answerable to the unworthiness of our disobedience; and therefore we needed one who was as great and worthy as we were unworthy.

Another objection (that perhaps may be thought hardly worth mentioning) is that to suppose sin to be infinitely heinous is to make all sins equally heinous; for how can sin be more than infinitely heinous? But all that can be argued from this is that no sin can be greater, with respect to that aggravation, than the worthiness of the object against whom it is committed. One sin cannot be more aggravated than another in that respect because the aggravation of every sin is infinite; but that does not hinder that some sins may be more heinous than others in other respects. If we supposed that a cylinder was infinitely long, it could not be greater in that respect, with respect to the length of it; yet it may be doubled and tripled, and made a thousandfold more, by the increase of other dimensions. Of sins that are all infinitely heinous, some may be more heinous than others.

This is true of various punishments that are all infinitely dreadful calamities, or all of them infinitely exceeding all finite calamities, so that there may be no finite calamity, however great, but is infinitely less dreadful or more eligible than any of these infinite ones, yet some of them may be a thousand times more dreadful than others. A punishment may be infinitely dreadful by reason of the infinite duration of it, and therefore cannot be greater with respect to that aggravation of it (its length of continuance); yet it may be vastly more terrible on other accounts.

As I have thus made it clear that all sin is infinitely heinous, and consequently that the sinner, before he is justified, is under infinite guilt in God's sight, it now remains that I show the consequence, or how it follows from hence that it is not suitable that God should give the sinner an interest in Christ's merits, and so a title to His benefits, from regard to any qualification, action, or course of actions in him, or on the account of any excellence or goodness whatsoever therein, but only as they unite him to Christ; or (which fully implies it) that it is not suitable that God, by any act, should, in any manner or degree, testify any acceptance of or pleasedness with anything—such as any virtue, excellence, or any part of loveliness or valuableness in his person—until he actually has an interest in Christ's merits.

From these premises it follows that before the sinner has an interest already in Christ and is justified, it is impossible that God should have any acceptance of or pleasedness with the person of the sinner so as, in any degree, to be lovely in His sight or less the object of His displeasure and wrath. For the sinner still remains infinitely guilty in the sight of God; for guilt is not removed but by pardon. But to suppose the sinner to be already pardoned is to suppose him to be already justified, which is contrary to the supposition. But if the sinner still remains infinitely guilty in God's sight, that is the same thing as still to be beheld of God as infinitely the object of His displeasure and wrath, or infinitely hateful in His eyes. And, if this is so, where is any room for anything in him to be accepted as valuable or acceptable in God's sight, or for any act of favor of any kind towards him, or any gift whatsoever to him, in testimony of God's respect to and acceptance of something in him as being lovely and pleasing?

If we suppose that a sinner could have faith, or some

other grace in his heart, and yet remain separate from
Christ, so that he is not looked upon as being in Christ
or having any relation to Him, it would not be fitting
that such true grace should be accepted of God as having any loveliness in the sight of God. If it should be
accepted as the loveliness of the person, that would be
to accept the person as in some degree lovely to God;
but this cannot be consistent with his still remaining
under infinite guilt or infinite unworthiness in God's
sight, which that goodness has no worthiness to balance. While God beholds the man as separate from
Christ, He must behold him as he is in himself. And so
his goodness cannot be beheld by God but as taken
with his guilt and hatefulness, and as put in the scales
with it. And so his goodness is nothing because there is
a finite item on the balance against an infinite one,
whose proportion to it is nothing.

In such a case, if the man is looked on as he is in
himself, the excess of the weight in one scale above another must be looked upon as the quality of the man.
These contraries being beheld together, one takes
from another as one number is subtracted from another, and the man must be looked upon in God's
sight according to the remainder. For here, by the supposition, all acts of grace or favor, in not imputing the
guilt as it is, are excluded because that supposes a degree of pardon, and that supposes justification, which
is contrary to what is supposed, which is that the sinner
is not already justified. And therefore things must be
taken strictly as they are; and so the man is still as infinitely unworthy and hateful in God's sight as he was
before, without diminution, because his goodness
bears no proportion to his unworthiness, and there-

fore, when taken together, is nothing.

Hence may be more clearly seen the force of that expression in the text of "believing on Him that justifieth the ungodly"; for though there is indeed something in man that is really and spiritually good prior to justification, yet there is nothing that is accepted as any godliness or excellence of the person till after justification. Goodness or loveliness of the person in the acceptance of God in any degree is not to be considered as prior, but posterior in the order and method of God's proceeding in this affair. Though a respect to the natural suitableness between such a qualification and such a state goes before justification, yet the acceptance even of faith as any goodness or loveliness in the believer follows justification. The goodness is, on the aforementioned account, justly looked upon as nothing until the man is justified; and therefore the man is respected in justification as in himself altogether hateful. Thus the nature of things will not admit of a man having an interest given him in the merits or benefits of a Savior on the account of anything as a righteousness, virtue, or excellence in him.

2. A divine constitution antecedent to that which establishes justification by a Savior (and indeed antecedent to any need of a Savior) stands in the way of it, that is, of that original constitution or law which man was put under. By this constitution the sinner is condemned because he is a violator of that law, and stands condemned until he actually has an interest in the Savior, through whom he is set at liberty from that condemnation. But to suppose that God gives a man an interest in Christ as a reward for his righteousness or virtue is inconsistent with his still remaining under

condemnation till he has an interest in Christ, because he supposes that the sinner's virtue is accepted, and he accepted for it, before he has an interest in Christ, inasmuch as an interest in Christ is given as a reward for his virtue. But the virtue must first be accepted before it is rewarded, and the man must first be accepted for his virtue before he is rewarded for it with so great and glorious a reward; for the very notion of a reward is some good bestowed in testimony of respect to and acceptance of virtue in the person rewarded.

It is inconsistent with the honor of the majesty of the King of heaven and earth to accept anything from a condemned malefactor, condemned by the justice of His own holy law, till that condemnation is removed. And then such acceptance is inconsistent with, and contradictory to, such remaining condemnation; for the law condemns him who violates it to be totally rejected and cast off by God. But how can a man continue under this condemnation, utterly rejected and cast off by God, and yet have his righteousness or virtue be accepted, and himself accepted on account of it, so as to have so glorious a reward as an interest in Christ bestowed as a testimony of that acceptance?

I know that the answer will be that we now are not subject to that constitution which mankind was at first put under, but that God, in mercy to mankind, has abolished that rigorous constitution, put us under a new law, and introduced a more mild constitution, and that, the former constitution or law itself not remaining, there is no need of supposing that the condemnation of it remains to stand in the way of the acceptance of our virtue. And, indeed, there is no other way of avoiding this difficulty. The condemnation of the law must stand in force against a man until he actually has an interest in the Savior who has satisfied and answered the law, so as effectually to prevent any acceptance of his virtue either before, or even in order to attain, such an interest unless the law or constitution itself is abolished.

But the scheme of those modern divines by whom this is maintained seems to contain a great deal of absurdity and self-contradiction. They hold that the old law given to Adam, which requires perfect obedience, is entirely repealed, and that instead of it we are put under a new law which requires no more than imperfect, sincere obedience in compliance with our poor, infirm, impotent circumstances since the Fall, whereby we are unable to perform that perfect obedience that was required by the first law. For they strenuously maintain that it would be unjust of God to require anything of us that is beyond our present power and ability to perform; yet they hold that Christ died to satisfy for the imperfections of our obedience so that our imperfect obedience might be accepted instead of perfect obedience.

Now I would ask, how can these things hang together? Of what law are these imperfections of our obedience a breach of? If they are a breach of no law, then they are not sins; and if they are not sins, what need is there of Christ's dying to satisfy for them? But if they are sins, and so the breach of some law, what law is it? They cannot be a breach of the new law of those divines, for that requires nothing other than imperfect obedience, or obedience with imperfections; and they cannot be a breach of the old law, for that, they say, is entirely abolished, and we never were under it—and we

cannot break a law that we never were under. They say
that it would not be just in God to exact of us perfect
obedience, because it would not be just in God to require more of us than we can perform in our present
state, and to punish us for failing in it. And therefore,
by their own scheme, the imperfections of our obedience do not deserve to be punished. What need is there,
therefore, of Christ's dying to satisfy for them? What
need is there of Christ's suffering to satisfy for that
which is no fault, and in its own nature deserves no suffering? What need is there of Christ's dying to enable
our imperfect obedience to be accepted when, according to their scheme, it would be unjust in itself that
anything other than imperfect obedience should be
required? What need is there of Christ's dying to make
way for God's accepting such an obedience, as it would
in itself be unjust in Him not to accept? Is there any
need of Christ's dying to persuade God not to do unjustly? If it is said that Christ died to satisfy that law for
us that we might not be under that law, but might be
delivered from it—that there might be room for us to
be under a more mild law—still I would inquire: what
need is there of Christ's dying that we might not be
under a law that (according to their scheme) it would
in itself be unjust that we should be under, because in
our present state we are not able to keep it? What need
is there of Christ's dying that we might not be under a
law that it would be unjust that we should be under,
whether Christ died or not?

ARGUMENT 2. Thus far I have argued principally
from reason and the nature of things. I proceed now to
the second argument, which is that this is a doctrine of

which the Holy Scriptures, the revelation that God has given us of His mind and will—by which alone we can ever come to know how those who have offended God can come to be accepted of Him and justified in his sight—are exceedingly full. The Apostle Paul abundantly teaches that we are justified by faith alone, without the works of the law. There is no one doctrine that he insists so much upon, and that he handles with so much distinctness, explaining, giving reasons, and answering objections, as this one.

Here it is not denied by any that the apostle asserts that we are justified by faith without the works of the law, because the words are express; but only it is said that we take his words wrongly and understand something by them which never entered into his heart, in that when he excludes "the works of the law" we understand him to be speaking of the whole law of God, or the rule which God has given mankind to walk by, whereas all that he intends is the ceremonial law.

Some who oppose this doctrine indeed say that the apostle sometimes means that it is by simply the first act of faith—that is, by heartily embracing the gospel without any preceding holy life—that persons are admitted into a justified state. But, they say, it is by a persevering obedience that they are continued in a justified state, and it is by this that they are finally justified. But this is the same thing as to say that a man, on his first embracing the gospel, is only conditionally justified and pardoned. To pardon sin is to free the sinner from the punishment of it, or from the eternal misery that is due for it. And therefore, if a person is pardoned or freed from this misery on his first embracing the gospel, and yet not finally freed, but his actual freedom still depends on some condition yet to be performed, it is inconceivable how he can be pardoned otherwise than conditionally; that is, he is not properly actually pardoned and freed from punishment, but only has God's promise that he shall be pardoned on future conditions. God promises him that, if he perseveres in obedience, he shall be finally pardoned or actually freed from hell.

This is to make just nothing at all of the apostle's great doctrine of justification by faith alone. Such a conditional pardon is no pardon or justification at all, any more than what all mankind have, whether they embrace the gospel or not! For they all have a promise of final justification on condition of future sincere obedience as much as he who embraces the gospel. But not to dispute about this, we will suppose that there may be something or other at the sinner's first embracing the gospel that may properly be called "justification" or "pardon," and yet that final justification, or real freedom from the punishment of sin, is still suspended on conditions hitherto unfulfilled. Yet they who hold that sinners are thus justified on embracing the gospel suppose that they are justified by this no otherwise than as it is a leading act of obedience, or at least as virtue and moral goodness in them, and therefore would be excluded by the apostle as much as any other virtue or obedience, if it is allowed that he means the moral law when he excludes works of the law. And therefore, if that point is yielded, that the apostle means the moral law and not only the ceremonial law, their whole scheme falls to the ground.

And because the issue of the whole argument from those texts in St. Paul's epistles depends on the deter-

mination of this point, I would be particular in dis-
cussing it.

Some of our opponents in this doctrine of justification, when they deny that by the law the apostle means
the moral law, or the whole rule of life which God has
given to mankind, seem to choose to express themselves thus: the apostle intends only the Mosaic dispensation. But this comes to just the same thing as if they
said that the apostle means only to exclude the works of
the ceremonial law; for when they say that it is intended only that we are not justified by the works of the
Mosaic dispensation, if they mean anything by it, it
must be that we are not justified by attending and observing what is Mosaic in that dispensation, or by what
was peculiar to it, and wherein it differed from the
Christian dispensation. This is the same as that which
is ceremonial and positive, and not moral, in that administration. So that this is what I have to disprove: the
apostle, when he speaks of works of the law in this affair, means only works of the ceremonial law, or those
observances that were peculiar to the Mosaic administration.

And here it must be noted that nobody disputes with
them whether the works of the ceremonial law are not
included, or whether the apostle does not particularly
argue against justification by circumcision and other
ceremonial observances. Rather, all that is in question
is whether, when he denies justification by works of the
law, he is to be understood only as referring to the ceremonial law, or whether the moral law is not also implied and intended. And therefore those arguments
which are brought to prove that the apostle meant the
ceremonial law prove nothing unless they prove that

the apostle meant those only.

What is much insisted on is that it was the judaizing Christians being so fond of circumcision and other ceremonies of the law, and depending so much on them, which was the very occasion of the apostle's writing, as he does against justification by the works of the law. But supposing it were so that their trusting in works of the ceremonial law was the sole occasion of the apostle's writing (which yet there is no reason to allow, as may appear afterwards)—if their trusting in a particular work as a work of righteousness was all that gave occasion to the apostle to write, how does it follow that therefore the apostle did not upon that occasion write against trusting in all works of righteousness whatsoever? Where is the absurdity of supposing that the apostle might take occasion from seeing some people trust in a certain work as a work of righteousness to write to them against persons trusting in any works of righteousness at all, and that it was a very proper occasion too? Yea, it would have been unavoidable for the apostle to have argued against trusting in a particular work, in the quality of a work of righteousness, which quality was general, without him therein arguing against trusting in works of righteousness in general.

Suppose that it had been some other particular sort of works that was the occasion of the apostle's writing, such as, for instance, works of charity; and suppose the apostle should hence take occasion to write to them not to trust in their works; could the apostle by that be understood as referring to no other works *besides* works of charity? Would it have been absurd to understand him as writing against trusting in any work at all because it was their trusting in a particular work that gave occasion to his writing?

Another thing alleged as evidence that the apostle means the ceremonial law when he says that we cannot be justified by the works of the law is that he uses this argument to prove it: the law he speaks of was given so long after the covenant with Abraham. Galatians 3:17: "And this I say, that the covenant, that was confirmed before of God in Christ, the law, which was four hundred and thirty years after, cannot disannul." But, say they, it was only the Mosaic administration, and not the covenant of works, that was given so long after. But they seem to manifestly mistake the apostle's argument.

The apostle does not speak of a law that began to exist four hundred and thirty years after. If he did, there would be some force in their objection; but he has respect to a certain solemn transaction, well known among the Jews by the phrase "the giving of the law," which was at Mount Sinai (Exodus 19–20), consisting especially in God's giving the Ten Commandments (which is the moral law) with a terrible voice, which law He afterwards gave in tables of stone.

This transaction the Jews in the apostle's time misinterpreted; they looked upon it as God's establishing that law as a rule of justification. Against this conceit of theirs the apostle brings this invincible argument: God would never annul His covenant with Abraham, which was plainly a covenant of grace, by a transaction with his posterity that was so long after it, and was plainly built upon it. He would not overthrow a covenant of grace that He had long before established with Abraham, for him and his seed (which is often mentioned as the ground of God's making them His peo-

ple), by now establishing a covenant of works with
them at Mount Sinai, as the Jews and judaizing Christians supposed.

But that the apostle does not mean only works of
the ceremonial law, when he excludes works of the law
in justification, but also the moral law, and all works of
obedience, virtue, and righteousness whatsoever, may
appear by the following things:

1. The apostle does not only say that we are not justified by the works of the law, but that we are not justified
by works, using a general term. We see this in our text:
"to him that worketh not, but believeth on Him that
justifieth." Romans 4:6: "God imputeth righteousness
without works." Romans 11:6: "And if by grace, then is it
no more of works, otherwise grace is no more grace;
but if it be of works, then it is no more grace; otherwise
work is no more work." Ephesians 2:8–9: "For by grace
are ye saved through faith, not of works." From all these
there is no reason in the world to understand the apostle to mean anything other than works in general as
correlates of a reward, or good works, or works of virtue
and righteousness.

When the apostle says we are not justified or saved
by works, without any such term annexed as "the law,"
or any other addition to limit the expression, what warrant does anyone have to confine it to works of a particular law or institution, excluding others? Are not observances of other divine laws works as well as observances of that one? It seems to be allowed by the divines
who accept the Arminian scheme, in their interpretation of several of those texts where the apostle mentions only works without any addition, that he means
our own good works in general; but then, they say, he

means only to exclude any proper merit in those works. But to say the apostle means one thing when he says that we are not justified by works, and another when he says that we are not justified by the works of the law, when we find the expressions mixed and used in the same discourse, and when the apostle is evidently upon the same argument, is very unreasonable. It is to dodge and fly from Scripture rather than to open and yield ourselves to its teachings.

2. In the third chapter of Romans, our having been guilty of breaches of the moral law is an argument that the apostle uses as to why we cannot be justified by the works of the law. Beginning with verse 9, he proves out of the Old Testament that all are under sin: "There is none righteous, no, not one; their throat is as an open sepulchre; with their tongues they have used deceit; their mouth is full of cursing and bitterness, and their feet swift to shed blood." And so he goes on, mentioning only those things that are breaches of the moral law. Then, when he has done this, his conclusion is, in verses 19–20: "Now we know that whatsoever things the law saith, it saith to them who are under the law, that every mouth may be stopped, and all the world may become guilty before God. Therefore, by the deeds of the law shall no flesh be justified in His sight."

This is most evidently his argument: because all had sinned (as was said in verse 9) and been guilty of those breaches of the moral law that he had mentioned (and it is repeated over again in verse 23: "For all have sinned, and come short of the glory of God"), therefore none at all can be justified by the deeds of the law. Now if the apostle meant only that we are not justified by the deeds of the ceremonial law, what kind of arguing

would that be? "Their mouth is full of cursing and bitterness, their feet are swift to shed blood"—and therefore they cannot be justified by the deeds of the Mosaic
administration? They are guilty of the breaches of the
moral law, and therefore they cannot be justified by the
deeds of the ceremonial law! Doubtless, the apostle's
argument is that the very same law they have broken
can never justify them as observers of it because every
law necessarily condemns its violators. And therefore
our breaches of the moral law argue simply that we
cannot be justified by the law that we have broken.

And it may be noted that the apostle's argument
here is the same that I have already used, that is, that as
we, in ourselves and outside of Christ, are under the
condemnation of that original law or constitution that
God established with mankind, therefore it is in no way
fitting that anything we do, any virtue or obedience of
ours, should be accepted, or that we should be accepted
on account of it.

3. The apostle, in all the preceding part of this epistle, wherever he has the phrase "the law," evidently intends the moral law principally. Romans 2:12: "For as
many as have sinned without law shall also perish
without law." He means the written moral law, as is evident by verses 14–15: "For when the Gentiles, which
have not the law, do by nature the things contained in
the law [that is, the moral law that the Gentiles have by
nature] which show the work of the law written in their
hearts." It is the moral law, and not the ceremonial,
that is written in the hearts of those who are destitute
of divine revelation.

And so in the 18th verse: "Thou approvest the things
that are more excellent, being instructed out of the

law." It is the moral law that shows us the nature of
things, and teaches us what is excellent. Verse 20:
"Thou hast a form of knowledge and truth in the law."
It is the moral law of which he speaks, as is evident by
what follows in verses 22–23: "Thou that sayest a man
should not commit adultery, dost thou commit adultery? Thou that abhorrest idols, dost thou commit sacrilege? Thou that makest thy boast of the law, through
breaking the law dishonorest thou God?" Adultery,
idolatry, and sacrilege are surely the breaking of the
moral law, not the ceremonial. So in verse 27: "And
shall not uncircumcision which is by nature, if it fulfill
the law, judge thee, who by the letter and circumcision
dost transgress the law?" In other words, he says, the
Gentiles, whom you despise because they are uncir-
cumcised, if they live moral and holy lives in obedience
to the moral law, shall condemn you though you are
circumcised. And so there is not one place in all the
preceding part of the epistle where the apostle speaks
of the law but where he most apparently intends principally the moral law; and yet when the apostle, in continuance of the same discourse, comes to tell us that we
cannot be justified by the works of the law, then they
will insist that he means only the ceremonial law. Yea,
all this discourse about the moral law, showing how the
Jews as well as Gentiles have violated it, is evidently
preparatory and introductory to that doctrine in
Romans 3:20, that "no flesh," that is, none of mankind,
neither Jews nor Gentiles, can be justified by the works
of the law.

4. It is evident that when the apostle says we cannot
be justified by the works of the law he means the moral
as well as ceremonial law, by his giving this reason for

it, that "by the law is the knowledge of sin" (Romans 3:20).

Now that law by which we come to the knowledge of sin is the moral law chiefly and primarily. If this argument of the apostle is good (that we cannot be justified by the deeds of the law, because it is by the law that we come to the knowledge of sin), then it proves that we cannot be justified by the deeds of the moral law, nor by the precepts of Christianity; for by them is the knowledge of sin. If the reason is good, then, where the reason holds, the truth holds. It is a miserable shift, and a violent force put upon the words, to say that the meaning is that by the law of circumcision comes the knowledge of sin, because circumcision, signifying the taking away of sin, puts men in mind of sin. The plain meaning of the apostle is that, as the law most strictly forbids sin, it tends to convince us of sin and bring our own consciences to condemn us instead of justifying us; the use of it is to declare to us our own guilt and unworthiness, which is the reverse of justifying and approving us as virtuous or worthy. This is the apostle's meaning, if we will allow him to be his own expositor; for he himself, in this very epistle, explains to us how it is that by the law we have the knowledge of sin, and that it is by the law's forbidding sin. Romans 7:7: "I had not known sin, but by the law; for I had not known lust, except the law had said, 'Thou shalt not covet.' "

Here the apostle determines two things: first, that the way in which "by the law is the knowledge of sin" is by the law's forbidding sin; and, second, which is more directly still to the purpose, he determines that it is the moral law by which we come to the knowledge of sin. "For," says he, "I had not known lust, except the law had said, 'Thou shalt not covet.' " Now it is the moral and not the ceremonial law that says, "Thou shalt not covet." Therefore, when the apostle argues that by the deeds of the law no flesh living shall be justified because by the law is the knowledge of sin, his argument proves (unless he was mistaken as to the force of his argument) that we cannot be justified by the deeds of the moral law.

5. It is evident that the apostle does not mean only the ceremonial law, because he gives this reason why we have righteousness and a title to the privilege of God's children: not by the law, but by faith, in that "the law worketh wrath." Romans 4:13–16: "For the promise that he should be the heir of the world was not to Abraham, or to his seed through the law, but through righteousness of faith. For if they which are of the law be heirs, faith is made void, and the promise made of none effect. Because the law worketh wrath; for where no law is, there is no transgression. Therefore it is of faith, that it might be by grace."

Now the way in which the law works wrath, by the apostle's own account in the reason he himself annexes, is by forbidding sin and aggravating the guilt of the transgression. "For," says he, "where no law is, there is no transgression." And so Romans 7:13 says that "sin by the commandment might become exceeding sinful." If, therefore, this reason of the apostle is good, it is much stronger against justification by the moral law than by the ceremonial law; for it is by transgressions of the moral law chiefly that there comes wrath—for they are most strictly forbidden, and most terribly threatened.

6. It is evident that, when the apostle says we are not

justified by the works of the law, he excludes all our own virtue, goodness, or excellence. This is evident by the reason he gives: that boasting might be excluded. Romans 3:26–28: "To declare, I say, at this time His righteousness; that He might be just, and the Justifier of him which believeth in Jesus. Where is boasting then? It is excluded. By what law? of works? Nay, but by the law of faith. Therefore we conclude that a man is justified by faith without the deeds of the law." Ephesians 2:8–9: "For by grace are ye saved through faith, and that not of yourselves; it is the gift of God, not of works, lest any man should boast." Now what are men wont to boast of but what they esteem their own goodness or excellence? If we are not justified by works of the ceremonial law, how does that exclude boasting, as long as we are justified by our own excellence, or virtue and goodness of our own, or works of righteousness which we have done?

But some answer that boasting is excluded as circumcision was excluded, which was what the Jews especially gloried in, and valued themselves above other nations.

I answer that the Jews were not only used to boasting of circumcision, but were notorious for boasting of their moral righteousness. The Jews of those days were generally admirers and followers of the Pharisees, who were full of boasts about their moral righteousness. We may see this by the example of the Pharisee mentioned in Luke 18, which Christ mentions as describing the general temper of that sect. "Lord," says he, "I thank Thee that I am not as other men, an extortioner, nor unjust, nor an adulterer." The works that he boasts of were chiefly moral works. He depended on the works of the law for justification. And therefore Christ tells us that the publican who renounced all his own righteousness "went down to his house justified rather than he."

And elsewhere we read of the Pharisees praying in the corners of the streets, and sounding a trumpet before them when they did alms. But those works which they so vainly boasted of were moral works. And not only so, but what the apostle in this very epistle condemns the Jews for is their boasting of the moral law. Romans 2:22–23: "Thou that sayest a man should not commit adultery, dost thou commit adultery? Thou that abhorrest idols, dost thou commit sacrilege? Thou that makest thy boast of the law, through breaking the law dishonorest thou God?" The law here mentioned that they made their boast of was that of which adultery, idolatry, and sacrilege were the breaches, which is the moral law.

So this is the boasting which the apostle condemns them for; and therefore, if they were justified by the works of this law, then how does he come to say that their boasting is excluded? And besides, when they boasted of the rites of the ceremonial law, it was under a notion of its being a part of their own goodness or excellence, or what made them holier and more lovely in the sight of God than other people. And if they were not justified by this part of their own supposed goodness or holiness, yet if they were by another, how did that exclude boasting? How was their boasting excluded unless *all* goodness or excellence of their own was excluded?

7. The next reason given by the apostle why we can be justified only by faith, and not by the works of the

law, comes in Galatians 3. When he says that "they that
are under the law are under the curse," he makes it evident that he does not mean only the ceremonial law. In
that chapter the apostle had particularly insisted that
Abraham was justified by faith, and that it is by faith
only, and not by the works of the law, that we can be
justified, become the children of Abraham, and be
made partakers of the blessing of Abraham. And he
gives this reason for it in verse 10: "For as many as are
of the works of the law are under the curse; for it is written, 'Cursed is everyone that continueth not in all
things which are written in the book of the law to do
them.' " It is manifest that these words, cited from
Deuteronomy, are spoken not only with regard to the
ceremonial law, but the whole law of God for mankind,
and chiefly the moral law; and that all mankind are
therefore, as they are in themselves, under that curse
not only while the ceremonial law lasted, but now since
that has ceased. And therefore all who are justified are
redeemed from that curse by Christ's bearing it for
them. Verse 13: "Christ hath redeemed us from the
curse of the law, being made a curse for us; for it is written, 'Cursed is everyone that hangeth on a tree.' " Now,
therefore, either its being said that he is cursed who
continues not in all things which are written in the
book of the law to do them is a good reason why we
cannot be justified by the works of that law of which it
is so said, or it is not. If it is, then it is a good reason
why we cannot be justified by the works of the moral
law, and of the whole rule which God has given to
mankind to walk by; for the words are spoken of the
moral as well as the ceremonial law, and reach every
command or precept which God has given to man-

kind—and chiefly the moral precepts which are most strictly enjoined, and the violations of which (in both the New Testament and the Old, and in the books of Moses themselves) are threatened with the most dreadful curse.

8. The apostle in like manner argues against our being justified by our own righteousness as he does against being justified by the works of the law; and he evidently uses the terms "of our own righteousness" and "works of the law" promiscuously, and as signifying the same thing. This is particularly evident by Romans 10:3: "For they being ignorant of God's righteousness, and going about to establish their own righteousness, have not submitted themselves unto the righteousness of God." Here it is plain that the same thing is asserted as in Romans 9:31–32: "But Israel, which followed after the law of righteousness, hath not attained to the law of righteousness. Wherefore? because they sought it not by faith, but as it were by the works of the law." And it is very unreasonable upon several accounts to suppose that the apostle, by "their own righteousness," intends only their ceremonial righteousness. For when the apostle warns us against trusting in our own righteousness for justification, doubtless it is fair to interpret the expression in an agreement with other scriptures where we are warned not to think that it is for the sake of our own righteousness that we obtain God's favor and blessing.

One text in particular is Deuteronomy 9:4–6: "Speak not thou in thine heart, after that the LORD thy God hast cast them out from before thee, saying, 'For my righteousness the LORD hath brought me in to possess this land'; but for the wickedness of these nations the

LORD doth drive them out from before thee. Not for thy
righteousness, or for the uprightness of thine heart,
dost thou go to possess their land, but for the wickedness of these nations the LORD thy God doth drive
them out from before thee, and that He may perform
the word which the LORD swore unto thy fathers,
Abraham, Isaac, and Jacob. Understand, therefore, that
the LORD thy God giveth thee not this good land to
possess it for thy righteousness; for thou art a stiff-
necked people." None will pretend that here the expression "thy righteousness" signifies only a ceremonial righteousness, but all virtue or goodness of their
own; yea, and the inward goodness of the heart as well
as the outward goodness of life. This appears by the beginning of verse 5: "Not for thy righteousness, or for
the uprightness of thy heart," and also by the antithesis
in verse 6: "Not for thy righteousness, for thou art a
stiff-necked people." Their stiff-neckedness was their
moral wickedness, obstinacy, and perverseness of heart.
By "righteousness," therefore, on the contrary, is meant
their moral virtue and rectitude of heart and life. I
would argue from hence that the expression "of our
own righteousness," when used in Scripture with relation to the favor of God—and when we are warned
against looking upon it as that by which that favor or
the fruits of it are obtained—does not signify only a
ceremonial righteousness, but all manner of goodness
of our own.

The Jews also, in the New Testament, are condemned for trusting in their own righteousness in this
sense. Luke 18:9: "And He spake this parable unto certain that trusted in themselves that they were righteous." This intends chiefly a moral righteousness, as

appears by the parable itself in which we have an account of the prayer of the Pharisee, wherein the things that he mentions as what he trusts in are chiefly moral qualifications and performances—that he was not an extortioner, unjust, nor an adulterer, and so on.

But we need not go to the writings of other penmen of the Scripture if we will allow the Apostle Paul to be his own interpreter. When Paul speaks of our own righteousness as that by which we are not justified or saved, he does not mean only a ceremonial righteousness, nor does he only intend a way of religion and serving God of our own choosing without divine warrant or prescription, but by "our own righteousness" he means the same as a righteousness of our own doing, whether it is a service or righteousness of God's prescribing or our own unwarranted performing. Let it be an obedience to the ceremonial law, or a gospel obedience, or what it will, if it is a righteousness of our own doing it is excluded by the apostle in this affair, as is evident by Titus 3:5: "Not by works of righteousness which we have done."

9. But I would more particularly insist on this text for my next argument that, when the apostle denies justification by works (works of the law and our own righteousness), he does not mean works of the ceremonial law only. Titus 3:3–7: "For we ourselves also were sometimes foolish, disobedient, deceived, serving divers lusts and pleasures, living in malice and envy, hateful, and hating one another. But after the kindness and love of God our Savior toward man appeared, not by works of righteousness which we have done, but according to His mercy He saved us, by the washing of regeneration and renewing of the Holy Ghost, which He shed on us

abundantly through Jesus Christ our Savior; that being justified by His grace we should be made heirs according to the hope of eternal life."

Works of righteousness that we have done are here excluded as being that by which we are neither saved nor justified. The apostle expressly says that we are not saved by them; and it is evident that when he says this he has respect to the issue of justification. He means that we are not saved by them in not being justified by them, as shown by Titus 3:7, which is part of the same sentence: "That being justified by His grace, we should be made heirs according to the hope of eternal life."

It is clear in several ways that the apostle in this text, by "works of righteousness which we have done," does not mean only works of the ceremonial law. It appears by the third verse: "For we ourselves also were sometimes foolish, disobedient, deceived, serving divers lusts and pleasures, living in malice and envy, hateful, and hating one another." These are breaches of the moral law that the apostle observes they lived in before they were justified; and it is most plain that it is this which gives occasion to the apostle to observe, as he does in the fifth verse, that it was not by works of righteousness which they had done that they were saved or justified.

But we need not go to the context; it is most apparent from the words themselves that the apostle does not mean only works of the ceremonial law. If he had only said, "It is not by our own works of righteousness," what could we understand by "works of righteousness" but only "righteous works," or, which is the same thing, "good works"? And to say that it is by our own righteous works that we are justified, though not by one particular kind of righteous works, would certainly be a contradiction to such an assertion. But the words are rendered yet more strong, plain, and determined in their sense by those additional words "which we have done," which shows that the apostle intends to exclude all our own righteous or virtuous works universally.

If it should be asserted, concerning any commodity, treasure, or precious jewel, that it could not be procured by money, and not only so but, to make the assertion more strong still, it should be asserted with additional words that it could not be procured by money that men possess—how unreasonable would it be, after all this, to say that all that was meant was that it could not be procured with brass money!

And what renders the interpreting of this text as intending works of the ceremonial law yet more unreasonable is that these works were indeed no works of righteousness at all, but were only falsely supposed to be so by the Jews. And this our opponents in this doctrine also suppose is the very reason why we are not justified by them, because they are not works of righteousness, or because (the ceremonial law being now abrogated) there is no obedience in them. But how absurd is it to say that the apostle, when he says we are not justified by works of righteousness that we have done, meant only works of the ceremonial law, and that for the very reason that these are not works of righteousness! Let me illustrate this by returning to the aforementioned comparison. If it should be asserted that such a thing could not be procured by money that men possess, how ridiculous would it be to say that the meaning only was that it could not be procured by counterfeit money, and that because such was not real money! What Scripture will stand before men if they

take liberty to manage Scripture thus? Or what one text
is there in the Bible that may not at this rate be explained away, and perverted to any sense men please?

But, further, if we should allow that the apostle intends only to oppose justification by works of the ceremonial law in this text, yet it is evident by the expression he uses that he means to oppose it under that notion, or in that quality, of their being works of righteousness of our own doing. But if the apostle argues
against our being justified by works of the ceremonial
law, under the notion of their being within the cate-
gory of works of our own doing, then it will follow that
the apostle's argument is strong against not only those,
but all of that nature and kind, indeed all that are of
our own doing.

If there were no other text in the Bible about justification but this, this would clearly and invincibly prove
that we are not justified by anything of our own goodness, virtue, or righteousness, or for the excellence or
righteousness of anything that we have done in religion, because it is here so fully and strongly asserted.
But this text abundantly confirms other texts of the
apostle where he denies justification by works of the
law. No doubt can be rationally made but that the apostle, when he shows that God does not save us by "works
of righteousness that we have done" (verse 5), and that
we are "justified by grace" (verse 7), herein opposing
salvation by works with salvation by grace, means the
same works as he does in other places where he in like
manner opposes works and grace. One such place is
Romans 11:6: "And if by grace, then it is no more of
works; otherwise grace is no more grace. But if it be of
works, then is it no more grace; otherwise work is no

more work."

These are the same works as are spoken of in Romans 4:4: "Now to him that worketh is the reward not reckoned of grace, but of debt." And these are the same works that are spoken of in the context of Romans 3:20, 24, which the apostle there calls "works of the law," saying we are "justified freely by His grace." And Romans 4:16: "Therefore it is of faith, that it might be by grace." In the context, the righteousness of faith is opposed to the righteousness of the law; for here God's saving us according to His mercy and justifying us by grace is opposed to saving us by works of righteousness that we have done. In the same manner as in those places, justifying us by His grace is opposed to justifying us by works of the law.

10. The apostle could not mean only works of the ceremonial law when he says that we are not justified by the works of the law, because it is asserted of the saints under the Old Testament as well as under the New. If men are justified by their sincere obedience, it will then follow that formerly, before the ceremonial law was abrogated, men were justified by the works of the ceremonial law as well as the moral. For if we are justified by our sincere obedience, then it does not alter the case whether the commands are moral or positive, provided that they are God's commands and our obedience is obedience to God.

And so the case must be just the same under the Old Testament, with the works of the moral and ceremonial law, according to the measure of the virtue of obedience there was in either. It is true, their obedience to the ceremonial law would have nothing to do with their justification unless it was sincere; and so neither would the works of the moral law. If obedience was the thing, then obedience to the ceremonial law, while that stood in force, and obedience to the moral law had equal significance, according to the proportion of obedience that consisted in each.

Now, under the New Testament, if obedience is what we are justified by, that obedience must doubtless comprehend obedience to all God's commands now in force—to the positive precepts of attendance on baptism and the Lord's Supper as well as moral precepts. If obedience is the thing, it is not because it is obedience to a certain kind of commands, but because it is obedience. Thus, by this supposition, the saints under the Old Testament were justified, at least in part, by their obedience to the ceremonial law.

But it is evident that the saints under the Old Testament were not justified in any measure by the works of the ceremonial law. This may be proven by proceeding on the foot of our adversaries' own interpretation of the apostle's phrase, "the works of the law," and supposing them to mean by it only the works of the ceremonial law. It is evident that David was not justified in any way by the works of the ceremonial law, as shown by Romans 4:6–8: "Even as David also describeth the blessedness of the man unto whom God imputeth righteousness without works, saying, 'Blessed are they whose iniquities are forgiven, and whose sins are covered. Blessed is the man to whom the Lord will not impute sin.' " It is plain that the apostle is here speaking of justification, from the preceding verse and from all the context; and the thing spoken of, forgiving iniquities and covering sins, is what our adversaries themselves suppose to be justification, and even the whole of

justification. This justification David, speaking of himself, says (by the apostle's interpretation) that he had
without works. For it is manifest that David, in the
words here cited, from the beginning of the 32nd
Psalm, has a special respect to himself. He speaks of his
own sins being forgiven and not imputed to him, as
appears by the words that immediately follow: "When I
kept silence, my bones waxed old through my roaring
all the day long. For day and night Thy hand was heavy
upon me; my moisture is turned into the drought of
summer. I acknowledged my sin unto Thee, and mine
iniquity have I not hid. I said, 'I will confess my transgressions unto the Lord'; and Thou forgavest the iniquity of my sin" (Psalm 32:3–5).

Thus, however we understand the apostle regarding
works, when he says, "David describes the blessedness
of the man to whom the Lord imputes righteousness
without works," whether it is of all manner of works or
only works of the ceremonial law, yet it is evident at
least that David was not justified by works of the ceremonial law.

Therefore here is the argument: if our own obedience is that by which men are justified, then under the
Old Testament men were justified partly by obedience
to the ceremonial law (as has been proven). But the
saints under the Old Testament were not justified partly
by the works of the ceremonial law. Therefore men's
own obedience is not that by which they are justified.

11. Another argument that the apostle, when he
speaks of the two opposite ways of justification—one by
the works of the law and the other by faith—does not
mean only the works of the ceremonial law, may be
taken from Romans 10:5–6: "For Moses describeth the

righteousness which is of the law, that the man which doeth those things shall live by them. But the righteousness which is of faith speaketh on this wise . . . ." Here two things are evident:

First, the apostle here speaks of the same two opposite ways of justification—one by the righteousness which is of the law, the other by faith—that he had treated in the former part of the epistle; and therefore it must be the same law that is here spoken of. The same law is here meant as in Romans 9:31–32,, where he says that the Jews had "not attained to the law of righteousness. Wherefore? Because they sought it not by faith, but as it were by the works of the law." This is plain because the apostle is still speaking of the same thing; the words are a continuation of the same discourse, as may be seen at first glance by anyone who looks at the context.

Second, it is manifest that Moses, when he describes the righteousness which is of the law, or the way of justification by the law, in the words here cited, "He that doeth those things shall live by them," does not speak only or chiefly of the works of the ceremonial law; for none will pretend that God ever made such a covenant with man that he who kept the ceremonial law should live in it, or that there ever was a time when it was chiefly by the works of the ceremonial law that men lived and were justified. Yea, it is manifest by the aforementioned instance of David, cited in Romans 4, that there never was a time wherein men were justified in any measure by the works of the ceremonial law, as has been just now shown.

Moses therefore, in those words which the apostle says are a description of the righteousness which is of the law, cannot mean only the ceremonial law. And therefore it follows that when the apostle speaks of justification by the works of the law as opposed to justification by faith, he does not mean only the ceremonial law, but also the works of the moral law, which are the things spoken of by Moses when he says, "He that doeth those things shall live by them." And these are the things which the apostle in this very place is arguing that we cannot be justified by, as is again evident by the last verses of the preceding chapter: "But Israel, which followed after the law of righteousness, hath not attained to the law of righteousness. Wherefore? Because they sought it, not by faith, but as it were by the works of the law." And also by Romans 10:3: "For they, being ignorant of God's righteousness, and going about to establish their own righteousness, have not submitted themselves unto the righteousness of God."

And, further, how can the apostle's description that he here gives of Moses, of this exploded way of justification by the works of the law, consist with the Arminian scheme, of a way of justification by the virtue of a sincere obedience that still remains as the true and only way of justification under the gospel? It is most apparent that it is the design of the apostle to give a description of both the legal (rejected) and the evangelical (valid) ways of justification, in that wherein they are distinguished each from the other. But how is it that "he who doeth those things shall live by them"— wherein the way of justification by the works of the law is distinguished from that in which Christians under the gospel are justified, according to their scheme? For still, according to them, it may be said, in the same manner, of the precepts of the gospel, "He who does

these things shall live by them." The difference lies
only in the things to be done, but not at all in that the
doing of them is not the condition of living in them,
just in the one case as in the other. The words "He that
doeth them shall live by them" will serve just as well for
a description of the latter as the former. By the apostle's saying that the righteousness of the law is described thus, "He who does these things shall live by
them; but the righteousness of faith says thus," he
plainly intimates that the righteousness of faith says
otherwise, and in an opposite manner. Besides, if these
words cited from Moses are actually said by him of the
moral law as well as the ceremonial, as it is most evident they are, this renders it still more absurd to suppose them to be mentioned by the apostle as the very
note of distinction between justification by a ceremonial obedience and a sincere moral obedience, as the
Arminians must suppose.

Thus I have spoken to a second argument, to prove
that we are not justified by any manner of virtue or
goodness of our own, and that to suppose otherwise is
contrary to the doctrine directly urged and abundantly
insisted on by the Apostle Paul in his epistles.

ARGUMENT 3. To suppose that we are justified by
our own sincere obedience, or anything of our own
virtue or goodness, derogates from gospel grace.

That scheme of justification which manifestly takes
from or diminishes the grace of God is undoubtedly to
be rejected; for it is the declared design of God in the
gospel to exalt the freedom and riches of His grace, in
that method of justifying sinners and that way of admitting them to His favor, and the blessed fruits of it

which it declares. The Scripture teaches that the way of justification appointed in the gospel covenant is appointed for the end that free grace might be expressed and glorified. Romans 4:16: "Therefore it is of faith, that it might be by grace." The exercising and magnifying of free grace in the gospel contrivance for the justification and salvation of sinners is evidently the chief design of it. And this freedom and riches of grace in the gospel are everywhere spoken of in Scripture as its chief glory. Therefore, as that doctrine which derogates from the free grace of God in justifying sinners is most opposed to God's design, so it must be exceedingly offensive to Him.

Those who maintain that we are justified by our own sincere obedience pretend that their scheme does not diminish the grace of the gospel; for, they say, the grace of God is wonderfully manifested in appointing such a way and method of salvation by sincere obedience, in assisting us to perform such an obedience, and in accepting our imperfect obedience instead of perfect obedience.

Let us therefore examine that matter, whether their scheme of a man's being justified by his own virtue and sincere obedience derogates from the grace of God or not, or whether free grace is not more exalted in supposing, as we do, that we are justified without any manner of goodness of our own. In order to accomplish this, I will lay down this self-evident proposition: whatsoever that is by which the abundant benevolence of the giver is expressed, and the gratitude in the receiver is obliged, magnifies free grace. I suppose that none would ever controvert or dispute this. And it is not much less evident that it shows both a more abundant

benevolence in the giver when he shows kindness
without goodness or excellence in the object to move
him to it, and that it enhances the obligation to gratitude in the receiver.

1. It shows a more abundant goodness in the giver
when he shows kindness without any excellence in our
persons or actions that should move the giver to love
and beneficence. For it certainly shows the more abundant and overflowing goodness, or disposition to
communicate good, by how much the less loveliness or
excellence there is to entice beneficence. The less
there is in the receiver to draw goodwill and kindness,
it argues the more of the principle of good will and
kindness in the giver. One who has but little of a principle of love and benevolence may be drawn to do good
and show kindness when there is a great deal to draw
him, or when there is much excellence and loveliness
in the object to move good will. On the other hand, he
whose goodness and benevolence is more abundant
will show kindness where there is less to draw it forth,
for he does not so much need to have it drawn from
outside him; he has enough of the principle within to
move him of itself. Where there is the most of the principle, there it is most sufficient for itself, and stands in
the least need of something outside to excite it. For certainly a more abundant goodness more easily flows
forth with less to impel or draw it than where there is
less; or, which is the same thing, the more anyone is
disposed of himself, the less he needs from outside
himself to put him upon it or stir him up to it. And
therefore his kindness and goodness appear more exceedingly great when they are bestowed without any excellence or loveliness at all in the receiver, or when the

receiver is respected in the gift as wholly without excellence—and much more still when the benevolence of the giver not only finds nothing in the receiver to draw it, but a great deal of hatefulness to repel it. The abundance of goodness is then manifested not only in flowing forth without anything extrinsic to put it forward, but in overcoming great repulsion in the object. And then kindness and love appear most triumphant and wonderfully great when the receiver is not only wholly without all excellence or beauty to attract it, but altogether, yea infinitely, vile and hateful.

2. It is apparent also that it enhances the obligation to gratitude in the receiver. It is agreeable to the common sense of mankind that the less worthy or excellent the object of benevolence or the receiver of kindness is, the more he is obliged and the greater gratitude is due. He therefore is most of all obligated who receives kindness without any goodness or excellence in himself, but with a total and universal hatefulness. And as it is agreeable to the common sense of mankind, so it is agreeable to the Word of God. How often does God in Scripture insist on this argument with men to move them to love Him and acknowledge His kindness! How much does He insist on this as an obligation to gratitude, that they are so sinful, undeserving, and ill-deserving!

Therefore it certainly follows that the doctrine which teaches that when God justifies a man, and shows him such great kindness as to give him a right to eternal life, He does not do it for any obedience or manner of goodness of his, but that justification respects a man as ungodly, and wholly without any manner of virtue, beauty, or excellence—I say, this doctrine

certainly more exalts the free grace of God in justification, and man's obligation to gratitude for such a favor,
than the contrary doctrine, which is that God, in showing this kindness to man, respects him as sincerely
obedient and virtuous, and as having something in
him that is truly excellent and lovely, and acceptable in
His sight, and that this goodness or excellence of man
is the very fundamental condition of the bestowal of
that kindness on him, or of distinguishing him from
others by that benefit.

ARGUMENT 4. To suppose a man is justified by his
own virtue or obedience derogates from the honor of
the Mediator, and ascribes that to man's virtue which
belongs only to the righteousness of Christ. It puts man
in Christ's stead and makes him his own savior in a respect in which Christ only is his Savior. And so it is a
doctrine contrary to the nature and design of the
gospel, which is to abase man and ascribe all the glory
of our salvation to Christ the Redeemer. It is inconsistent with the doctrine of the imputation of Christ's
righteousness, which is a gospel doctrine.

Here I would explain what we mean by the imputation of Christ's righteousness, prove the thing intended by it to be true, and show that this doctrine is utterly inconsistent with the doctrine of our being justified by our own virtue or sincere obedience.

First, I would explain what we mean by the imputation of Christ's righteousness. Sometimes the expression is taken by our divines in a larger sense, for the
imputation of all that Christ did and suffered for our
redemption whereby we are freed from guilt and stand
as righteous in the sight of God. And so it implies the

imputation of both Christ's satisfaction and His obedience. But I intend it in a stricter sense, for the imputation of that righteousness or moral goodness that consists in the obedience of Christ. And by that righteousness being imputed to us is meant nothing other than that the righteousness of Christ is accepted for us, and admitted instead of that perfect inherent righteousness which ought to be in ourselves. Christ's perfect obedience shall be reckoned to our account so that we shall have the benefit of it, as though we had performed it ourselves. And so we suppose that a title to eternal life is given us as the reward of this righteousness.

The Scripture uses the word "impute" in this sense: for reckoning anything belonging to any person to another person's account. Philemon 18: "If he hath wronged thee, or oweth thee ought, put that on mine account." In the original it is "impute that to me." It has the same root as that word which is translated "impute" in Romans 4:6: "Unto whom God imputeth righteousness without works." And it is the very same word that is used in Romans 5:13: "Sin is not imputed when there is no law."

The opposers of this doctrine suppose that there is an absurdity in supposing that God imputes Christ's obedience to us, in that it is to suppose that God is mistaken and thinks that we performed that obedience which Christ performed. But why cannot that righteousness be reckoned to our account and be accepted for us without any such absurdity? Why is there any more absurdity in it than in a merchant's transferring debt or credit from one man's account to another, when one man pays a price for another, so that it shall be accepted as if that other had paid it? Why is there

any more absurdity in supposing that Christ's obedience is imputed to us than that His satisfaction is imputed? If Christ has suffered the penalty of the law in
our stead, then it will follow that His suffering that
penalty is imputed to us, that it is accepted for us and in
our stead, and is reckoned to our account as though we
had suffered it. But why may not His obeying the law of
God be as rationally reckoned to our account as His
suffering the penalty of the law? Why may not a price to
bring into debt be as rationally transferred from one
person's account to another as a price to pay a debt?

Having thus explained what we mean by the imputation of Christ's righteousness, I proceed, second, to
prove that the righteousness of Christ is thus imputed.

1. There is the very same need of Christ's obeying
the law in our stead in order for us to obtain the reward
as of His suffering the penalty of the law in our stead in
order for us to escape the penalty—and the same reason why one should be accepted on our account as the
other. There is the same need of one as the other, that
the law of God might be answered. One was as requisite
to answer the law as the other. It is certain that the reason why Christ must suffer the penalty for us was that
the law might be answered; this the Scripture plainly
teaches. This is given as the reason why Christ was
made a curse for us, that the law threatened a curse to
us (Galatians 3:10, 13). But the same law that fixes the
curse of God as the consequence of not continuing in
all things written in the law to do them (verse 10) has,
just as much, fixed doing those things as an antecedent
of living in them (verse 12). There is as much connection established in one case as in the other. There is
therefore exactly the same need, from the law, of per-

fect obedience being fulfilled in order for us to obtain
the reward as there is of death being suffered in order
for us to escape the punishment; in other words, there
is the same necessity, by the law, of perfect obedience
preceding life as there is of disobedience being suc-
ceeded by death. The law is, without doubt, as much of
an established rule in one case as in the other.

Christ, by suffering the penalty, and so making
atonement for us, only removes the guilt of our sins,
and so sets us in the same state in which Adam was in
the first moment of his creation; and it is no more fitting that we should obtain eternal life only on that account than that Adam should have the reward of eternal life, or of a confirmed and unalterable state of happiness, in the first moments of his existence without
any obedience at all. Adam was not to have the reward
merely on account of his being innocent; if so, he
would have had it fixed upon him as soon as he was
created, for he was as innocent then as he could be. But
he was to have the reward on account of his activeness
in obedience—not on account merely of his not having
done ill, but on account of his doing well.

So on the same account we do not have eternal life
merely because we are devoid of guilt, which we are by
the atonement of Christ, but because of Christ's activeness in obedience and doing well. Christ is our second
federal head, and is called the second Adam
(1 Corinthians 15:22) because He acted that part for us
which the first Adam should have done. When He undertook to stand in our stead, He was looked upon and
treated as though He were guilty with our guilt. And by
His bearing the penalty, He did, as it were, free Himself
from this guilt. But by this the second Adam only

brought Himself into the state in which the first Adam was on the first moment of his existence: a state of mere freedom from guilt. And hereby, indeed, He was free from any obligation to suffer punishment; but this being supposed, there was need of something further, even a positive obedience, in order for Him to obtain, as our second Adam, the reward of eternal life.

God saw fit to place man first in a state of trial, and not to give him a title to eternal life as soon as He had made him, because it was His will that he should first give honor to His authority by fully submitting to it in will and act, and perfectly obeying His law. God insisted that His holy majesty and law should have their due acknowledgment and honor from man, such as befitted the relation he stood in to that Being who created him, before He would bestow the reward of confirmed and everlasting happiness upon him. And therefore God gave him a law that he might have opportunity, by giving due honor to His authority in obeying it, to obtain this happiness. It therefore became Christ—seeing that, in assuming manhood to Himself, He sought a title to this eternal happiness for him after he had broken the law—that He Himself should become subject to God's authority, and be in the form of a servant, so that He might do that honor to God's authority for man by His obedience which God at first required of man as the condition of his having a title to that reward.

Christ came into the world to render the honor of God's authority and law consistent with the salvation and eternal life of sinners. He came to save them, and yet withal to assert and vindicate the honor of the Lawgiver and His holy law. Now, if the sinner, after his sin was satisfied for, had eternal life bestowed upon him without active righteousness, the honor of His law would not be sufficiently vindicated. Suppose that it were possible that the sinner himself could, by suffering, pay the debt, and afterwards be in the same state that he was in before his probation, that is to say, negatively righteous, or merely without guilt; if he now at last should have eternal life bestowed upon him without performing that condition of obedience, then God would recede from His law, and would give the promised reward, and His law would never have respect and honor shown to it in that way of being obeyed. But now Christ, by subjecting Himself to the law and obeying it, has done great honor to the law, and to the authority of God who gave it. That so glorious a Person should become subject to the law and fulfill it has done much more to honor it than if mere man had obeyed it. It was a thing infinitely honorable to God that a Person of infinite dignity was not ashamed to call Him His God, and to adore and obey Him as such. This was more to God's honor than if any mere creature, of any possible degree of excellence and dignity, had done so.

It is absolutely necessary that, in order for a sin to be justified, the righteousness of some other should be reckoned to his account; for it is declared that the person justified is looked upon as (in himself) ungodly. But God neither will nor can justify a person without righteousness; for "justification" is manifestly a forensic term, as the word is used in Scripture, and a judicial thing, or the act of a judge. So that if a person should be justified without a righteousness, the judgment would not be according to truth. The sentence of justification would be a false sentence unless there was a righteousness performed that the judge properly could

look upon as his. To say that God does not justify the
sinner without sincere, though imperfect, obedience
does not help the case; for an imperfect righteousness
before a judge is no righteousness. To accept something that falls short of the rule instead of something
else that answers the rule is no judicial act, or act of a
judge, but a pure act of sovereignty. And imperfect righteousness is no righteousness before a judge; for
"righteousness (as one observes) is a relative thing, and
always has relation to a law. The formal nature of righteousness, properly understood, lies in a conformity of
actions to that which is the rule and measure of them."
Therefore that only is righteousness in the sight of a
judge that answers the law.

The law is the judge's rule. If he pardons and hides
what really is, and so does not pass sentence according
to what things are in themselves, he either does not act
the part of a judge or else judges falsely. The very notion of judging is to determine what is and what is not
in anyone's case. The judge's work is twofold: it is to
determine, first, what is fact, and then whether what is
in fact is according to rule or according to the law. If a
judge has no rule or law established beforehand by
which he should proceed in judging, he has no foundation to go upon in judging; he has no opportunity to
be a judge, nor is it possible that he should do the part
of a judge. To judge without a law or rule by which to
judge is impossible, for the very notion of judging is to
determine whether the object of judgment is according
to rule. And therefore God has declared that when He
acts as a judge He will not justify the wicked and cannot
clear the guilty. And, by parity of reason, He cannot justify without righteousness.

And the scheme of the old law's being abrogated and a new law introduced will not help at all in this difficulty, for an imperfect righteousness cannot answer the law of God we are under, whether that is an old or a new one. Every law requires perfect obedience to itself, and every rule whatsoever requires perfect conformity to itself; it is a contradiction to suppose otherwise. For to say that there is a law that does not require perfect obedience to itself is to say that there is a law that does not require all that it requires. That law which now forbids sin is certainly the law that we are now under (let that be an old or a new one), or else it is not sin. That which is not forbidden, and is the breach of no law, is no sin. But if we are now forbidden to commit sin, then it is by a law that we are now under; for surely we are neither under the forbiddings nor commands of a law that we are not under. Therefore, if all sin is now forbidden, then we are now under a law that requires perfect obedience; and therefore nothing can be accepted as a righteousness in the sight of our Judge but perfect righteousness. So that our Judge cannot justify us unless He sees a perfect righteousness, in some way belonging to us, either performed by ourselves or by another, and justly and duly reckoned to our account.

God, in the sentence of justification, pronounces a man perfectly righteous, or else he would need a further justification after he is justified. His sins being removed by Christ's atonement is not sufficient for a man's justification; for justifying a man, as has been already shown, is pronouncing him not merely innocent or without guilt, but standing right with regard to the rule that he is under, and righteous unto life. But this, according to the established rule of nature, reason, and divine appointment, is a positive, perfect righteousness. As there is the same need that Christ's obedience should be reckoned to our account as that His atonement should, so there is the same reason why it should. If Adam had persevered and finished his course of obedience, we would have received the benefit of his obedience as much as now we have the mischief of his disobedience. And in like manner, there is reason that we should receive the benefit of the second Adam's obedience as of his atonement for our disobedience. Believers are represented in Scripture as being so in Christ that they are legally one, or accepted as one, by the supreme Judge. Christ has assumed our nature, and has so assumed all in that nature that belongs to Him, into such a union with Himself, that He has become their Head, and has taken them to be His members. And therefore, what Christ has done in our nature, whereby He did honor to the law and authority of God by His acts, as well as the reparation to the honor of the law by His sufferings, is reckoned to the believer's account so that the believer should be made happy, because it was so well and worthily done by his Head, as well as freed from being miserable, because He has suffered for our ill and unworthy doing.

When Christ had undertaken with God to stand for us, and put Himself under our law, by that law He was obliged to suffer; and by the same law He was obliged to obey. By the same law, after He had taken man's guilt upon Him, He Himself, being our Surety, could not be acquitted until He had suffered, nor could He be rewarded until He had obeyed. But He was not acquitted as a private person, but as our Head, and believers are acquitted in His acquittal; nor was He accepted to a reward for His obedience as a private person, but as our Head, and we are accepted to a reward in His acceptance.

The Scripture teaches us that when Christ was raised from the dead, He was justified; and this justification, as I have already shown, implies both His acquittal from our guilt and His acceptance to the exaltation and glory that was the reward of His obedience. But believers, as soon as they believe, are admitted to partake with Christ in His justification. Hence we are told that He was "raised again for our justification" (Romans 4:25), which is true not only of that part of His justification that consists in His acquittal, but also His acceptance to His reward. The Scripture teaches us that He is exalted, and gone to heaven to take possession of glory in our name as our forerunner (Hebrews 6:20). We are, as it were, both raised up together with Christ, and also made to sit together with Christ in heavenly places, and in Him (Ephesians 2:6).

If it is objected here that there is a reason why what Christ suffered should be accepted on our account rather than the obedience He performed—namely, that He was obliged to obedience for Himself, but was not obliged to suffer but only on our account—to this I answer that Christ was not obliged on His own account to undertake to obey. In His original circumstances, Christ was in no subjection to the Father, being altogether equal with Him. He was under no obligation to put Himself in man's stead and under man's law, or to put Himself into any state of subjection to God whatsoever. There was a transaction between the Father and the Son that was antecedent to Christ's becoming man and being made under the law, wherein He undertook

to put Himself under the law, and both to obey and to
suffer. In this transaction these things were already virtually done in the sight of God, as is evident in that
God acted on the ground of that transaction, justifying
and saving sinners, as if the things undertaken had
been actually performed long before they were performed indeed. And therefore, without doubt, in order
to estimate the value and validity of what Christ did and
suffered, we must look back to that transaction wherein
these things were first undertaken, and virtually done
in the sight of God, and see what capacity and circumstances Christ fulfilled in them, and we shall find that
Christ was under no manner of obligation either to
obey the law or to suffer its penalty. After this He was
equally under obligation to both; for henceforward He
stood as our Surety or Representative. And therefore
this consequent obligation may be as much of an objection against the validity of His suffering the penalty
as against His obedience. But if we look to that original
transaction between the Father and the Son, wherein
both of these were undertaken and accepted as virtually
done in the sight of the Father, we shall find Christ acting with regard to both, as one perfectly in His own
right, and under no manner of previous obligation to
hinder the validity of either.

2. To suppose that all Christ does is only to make
atonement for us by suffering is to make Him our
Savior but in part. It is to rob Him of half His glory as a
Savior. For if all He does is to deliver us from hell, He
does not purchase heaven for us. The adverse scheme
supposes that He purchases heaven for us in that He
satisfies for the imperfections of our obedience, and so
purchases that our sincere imperfect obedience might

be accepted as the condition of eternal life, as well as purchasing an opportunity for us to obtain heaven by our own obedience. But to purchase heaven for us only in this sense is to purchase it in no sense at all; for all of it comes to no more than a satisfaction for our sins, or removing the penalty by suffering in our stead. For all the purchasing they speak of (that our imperfect obedience should be accepted) is only His satisfying for the sinful imperfection of our obedience, or (which is the same thing) making atonement for the sin which attends our obedience. But that is not purchasing heaven, when it merely sets us at liberty again, that we may go and get heaven by what we do ourselves. All that Christ does is to pay a debt for us; there is no positive purchase of any good.

We are taught in Scripture that heaven is purchased for us; it is called the purchased possession (Ephesians 1:14). The gospel proposes the eternal inheritance not to be acquired, as the first covenant did, but as already acquired and purchased. But he who pays a man's debt for him, and so delivers him from slavery, cannot be said to purchase an estate for him merely because he sets him at liberty so that henceforth he has an opportunity to get an estate by his own labor. So that, according to this scheme, the saints in heaven have no reason to thank Christ for purchasing heaven for them, or redeeming them to God, and making them kings and priests, as we have an account that they do in Revelation 5:9–10.

3. Justification by the righteousness and obedience of Christ is a doctrine that the Scripture teaches in very full terms. Romans 5:18–19: "By the righteousness of one, the free gift came upon all men unto justification

of life. For as by one man's disobedience many were
made sinners, so by the obedience of one shall many be
made righteous." Here in one verse we are told that we
have justification by Christ's righteousness; and, that
there might be no room to understand the righteousness spoken of merely as referring to Christ's atonement by His suffering the penalty, in the next verse it is
put in other terms, and asserted that it is by Christ's
obedience that we are made righteous. It is scarcely
possible that anything could be more full and determined. The terms, taken singly, are such that they fix
their own meaning; and taken together they fix the
meaning of each other. The words show that we are justified by that righteousness of Christ's which consists
in His obedience, and that we are made righteous or
justified by that obedience of His, that is, His righteousness or moral goodness before God.

Here it may be objected that this text means only
that we are justified by Christ's passive obedience.

I answer that, whether we call it active or passive, it
does not alter the case as to the present argument, as
long as it is evident by the words that it is not merely
under the notion of an atonement for disobedience or
a satisfaction for unrighteousness, but under the notion of positive obedience and righteousness (or moral
goodness) that Christ's action justifies us or makes us
righteous; for both the words "righteousness" and
"obedience" are used, and used too as the opposites of
sin, disobedience, and an offense. "Therefore, as by the
offense of one, judgment came upon all men to condemnation, even so, by the righteousness of one, the
free gift came upon all men to justification of life. For
as by one man's disobedience many were made sinners,

so, by the obedience of one, shall many be made righteous." Now, what can be meant by righteousness, when spoken of as the opposite of sin or moral evil, but moral goodness? What is the righteousness that is the opposite of an offense but the behavior that is well-pleasing? And what can be meant by obedience, when spoken of as the opposite of disobedience or going contrary to a command, but a positive obeying and an actual complying with the command? So there is no room for any invented distinction of active and passive to hurt the argument from this Scripture; for it is as evident by it as anything can be that believers are justified by the righteousness and obedience of Christ under the notion of His moral goodness—His positive obeying and actual complying with the commands of God—and that behavior which, because of its conformity to His commands, was well-pleasing in His sight. This is all that ever anyone needs to desire to have granted in this dispute.

By this it appears that if Christ's dying is here included in the words "righteousness" and "obedience," it is not merely as a propitiation, or bearing a penalty of a broken law in our stead, but as His voluntarily submitting and yielding Himself to those sufferings in obedience to the Father's commands, and so as a part of His positive righteousness or moral goodness.

Indeed, all obedience considered under the notion of righteousness is something active, something done in voluntary compliance with a command, whether it may be done without suffering or whether it is hard and difficult. Yet as it is obedience, righteousness, or moral goodness, it must be considered as something voluntary and active. If anyone is commanded to go through difficulties and sufferings, and he, in compliance with this command, voluntarily does it, he properly obeys in so doing. And as he voluntarily does it in compliance with a command, his obedience is as active as any whatsoever. It is the same sort of obedience, a thing of the very same nature, as when a man, in compliance with a command, does a piece of hard service, or goes through hard labor; and there is no room to distinguish between these types of obedience, as if they were of quite different natures, by such opposite terms as "active" and "passive." All the distinction that can be pretended is that between obeying an easy command and a difficult one. But is there from hence any foundation to make two species of obedience, one active and the other passive? There is no appearance of any such distinction ever entering into the hearts of any of the penmen of Scripture.

It is true that of late, when a man refuses to obey the precept of a human law, but patiently yields himself up to suffer the penalty of the law, it is called "passive obedience"; but this I suppose is only a modern use of the word "obedience." Surely it is a sense of the word to which the Scripture is a perfect stranger. It is improperly called "obedience," unless there is such a precept in the law that he shall yield himself patiently to suffer, to which his so doing shall be an active, voluntary conformity. There may in some sense be said to be a conformity to the law in a person's suffering the penalty of the law; but no other conformity to the law is properly called "obedience" to it except active, voluntary conformity to the precepts of it. The word "obey" is often found in Scripture with respect to the law of God for man, but never in any other sense.

It is true that Christ's willingly undergoing those sufferings which He endured is a great part of that obedience or righteousness by which we are justified. The sufferings of Christ are respected in Scripture under a twofold consideration: either merely as His being substituted for us or put into our stead in suffering the penalty of the law (and so His sufferings are considered as a satisfaction and propitiation for sin), or as He, in obedience to a law or command of the Father, voluntarily submitted Himself to those sufferings and actively yielded Himself up to bear them. And so they are considered as His righteousness and a part of His active obedience.

Christ underwent death in obedience to the command of the Father. Psalm 40:6–8: "Sacrifice and offering Thou didst not desire; mine ears hast Thou opened; burnt offering and sin offering hast Thou not required. Then said I, 'Lo, I come; in the volume of the book it is written of me, "I delight to do Thy will, O my God"; yea, Thy law is within my heart.' " John 10:17–18: "I lay down My life that I might take it again. No man taketh it from Me, but I lay it down of Myself. I have power to lay it down, and I have power to take it again. This commandment have I received of My Father." John 18:11: "The cup which My Father hath given Me, shall I not drink it?" And this is a part, and, indeed, the principal part of that active obedience by which we are justified.

It can be no just objection against this that the command of the Father to Christ that He should lay down His life was no part of the law that we had broken, and therefore that His obeying this command could be no part of that obedience that He performed for us because we needed Him to obey no other law for us but that which we had broken or failed to obey. For although it must be the same legislative authority whose honor is repaired by Christ's obedience that we have injured by our disobedience, yet there is no need that the law which Christ obeys should be precisely the same that Adam was to have obeyed, in the sense that there should be no positive precepts wanting, nor any added. There was wanting the precept about the forbidden fruit, and there was added the ceremonial law. The thing required was perfect obedience. It is no matter whether the positive precepts were the same, if they were equivalent.

The positive precepts that Christ was to obey were much more than equivalent to what was wanting, because they were infinitely more difficult, particularly the command that He had received to lay down His life, which was His principal act of obedience, and which, above all others, is concerned in our justification. As that act of disobedience by which we fell was disobedience to a positive precept that Christ never was under—that of abstaining from the tree of knowledge of good and evil—so that act of obedience by which principally we are redeemed is obedience to a positive precept that Adam never was under—the precept of laying down His life.

It was suitable that it should be a positive precept that would try both Adam's and Christ's obedience. Such precepts are the greatest and most proper trial of obedience because, in them, the mere authority and will of the legislator is the sole ground of the obligation (and nothing in the nature of the things themselves), and therefore they are the greatest trial of any person's respect for that authority and will.

The law that Christ was subject to, and which He obeyed, was in some sense the same that was given to Adam. There are innumerable particular duties required by the law only conditionally; and in such circumstances these are comprehended in some great and general rule of that law. Thus, for instance, there are innumerable acts of respect and obedience to men which are required by the law of nature (which was a law given to Adam) yet which are not required absolutely, but upon many prerequisite conditions—such as that there are men standing in certain relations to us, and that they give forth certain commands, and the like. So many acts of respect and obedience to God are included, in like manner, in the moral law conditionally, or such and such things being supposed: as Abraham's going about to sacrifice his son, the Jews' circumcising their children when they were eight days old, and Adam's not eating the forbidden fruit. They are virtually comprehended in that great general rule of the moral law, that we should obey God and be subject to Him in whatsoever He pleases to command us.

Certainly the moral law requires us to obey God's positive commands as much as it requires us to obey the positive commands of our parents. And thus all that Adam and Christ were commanded, even Christ's observing the rites and ceremonies of the Jewish worship and His laying down His life, was virtually included in this same great law.

It is no objection against the last-mentioned thing (Christ's laying down His life) that it was not included in the moral law given to Adam, because that law itself allowed of no occasion for any such thing; for the moral law virtually includes all right acts on all possible occasions, even occasions that the law itself does not allow. Thus we are obliged by the moral law to mortify our lusts and repent of our sins, though that law allows of no lust to mortify or sin to repent of.

There is indeed but one great law of God, and that is the same law that says, "if thou sinnest, thou shalt die," and "cursed is everyone that continues not in all things contained in this law to do them." All duties of positive institution are virtually comprehended in this law: and therefore, if the Jews broke the ceremonial law, this breach exposed them to the penalty of the law or covenant of works, which threatened, "thou shalt surely die." The law is the eternal and unalterable rule of righteousness between God and man, and therefore is the rule of judgment by which all that a man does shall be either justified or condemned—and no sin exposes to damnation but by the law. So now he who refuses to obey the precepts that require an attendance on the sacraments of the New Testament is exposed to damnation by virtue of the law or covenant of works.

It may moreover be argued that all sins whatsoever are breaches of the law or covenant of works because all sins, even breaches of the positive precepts as well as others, have atonement by the death of Christ; but what Christ died for was to satisfy the law, or to bear the curse of the law, as appears by Galatians 3:10–13 and Romans 8:3–4.

So Christ's laying down His life might be part of that obedience by which we are justified, though it was a positive precept not given to Adam. It was doubtless Christ's main act of obedience because it was obedience to a command that was attended with immensely the greatest difficulty, and so to a command that was the greatest trial of His obedience. The respect He showed to God in it, and His honoring God's authority, was proportionally great. It is spoken of in Scripture as Christ's principal act of obedience. Philippians 2:7–8: "But He made Himself of no reputation, and took upon Him the form of a servant, and was made in the likeness of men; and being found in fashion as a man, He humbled Himself, and became obedient unto death, even the death of the cross." Hebrews 5:8: "Though He were a Son, yet learned He obedience by the things which He suffered."

It was mainly by this act of obedience that Christ purchased so glorious a reward for Himself. Philippians 2:8–9: "He became obedient unto death, even the death of the cross. Wherefore God also hath highly exalted Him, and given Him a name which is above every name." And it therefore follows from what has been already said that it is mainly by this act of obedience that believers in Christ also have the reward of glory, or come to partake with Christ in His glory. We are as much saved by the death of Christ because His yielding Himself to die was an act of obedience as we are saved because it was a propitiation for our sins; for as it was not the only act of obedience that carried merit (He having performed meritorious acts of obedience through the whole course of His life), so neither was it the only suffering that was propitiatory. All His sufferings through the whole course of His life were propitiatory, just as every act of obedience was meritorious. Indeed, this was His principal suffering, and it was as much His principal act of obedience.

Hence we may see how the death of Christ not only

made atonement, but also merited eternal life; and hence we may see how, by the blood of Christ, we are not only redeemed from sin, but redeemed unto God. And therefore the Scripture seems everywhere to attribute the whole of salvation to the blood of Christ. This precious blood is as much the main price by which heaven is purchased as it is the main price by which we are redeemed from hell. The positive righteousness of Christ, or that price by which He earned merit, was of equal value with that by which He provided satisfaction; for indeed it was the same price. He spilled His blood to satisfy, and, by reason of the infinite dignity of His person, His sufferings were looked upon as of infinite value, and equivalent to the eternal sufferings of a finite creature. And He spilled His blood out of respect for the honor of God's majesty, and in submission to His authority, who had commanded Him to do so; and His obedience therein was of infinite value, both because of the dignity of the person who performed it and because He put Himself to infinite expense to perform it, whereby the infinite degree of His regard for God's authority appeared.

One would wonder what Arminians mean by "Christ's merits." They talk of Christ's merits as much as anybody, and yet deny the imputation of Christ's positive righteousness. What should there be that anyone should merit or deserve anything by, besides righteousness or goodness? If anything that Christ did or suffered merited or deserved anything, it was by virtue of the goodness, righteousness, or holiness of it. If Christ's sufferings and death merited heaven, it must be because there was an excellent righteousness and transcendent moral goodness in that act of laying down His life. And if by that excellent righteousness He merited heaven for us, then surely that righteousness is reckoned to our account so that we have the benefit of it, or, which is the same thing, it is imputed to us.

Thus, I hope, I have made it evident that the righteousness of Christ is indeed imputed to us.

3. I proceed now to the third and last point under this argument: that this doctrine of the imputation of Christ's righteousness is utterly inconsistent with the doctrine of our being justified by our own virtue or sincere obedience. If acceptance into God's favor and a title of life is given to believers as the reward of Christ's obedience, then it is not given to us as the reward of our own obedience. In whatever respect Christ is our Savior, that doubtless excludes our being our own saviors in that same respect. If we can be our own saviors in the same respect as Christ is, it would thence follow, that the salvation of Christ is needless in that respect. This is according to the apostle's reasoning in Galatians 5:4: "Christ is become of no effect unto you, whosoever of you are justified by the law." Doubtless, it is Christ's prerogative to be our Savior in that sense wherein He is our Savior. Therefore, if it is by His obedience that we are justified, then it is not by our own obedience.

Here, perhaps, it might be said that a title to salvation is not directly given as the reward of our obedience; for that is not by anything of ours, but only by Christ's satisfaction and righteousness. Yet an interest in that satisfaction and righteousness, one might argue, is given to us as a reward of our obedience.

But this does not at all help the case, for this is to ascribe as much to our obedience as if we ascribed sal-

vation to it directly, without the intervention of Christ's
righteousness. For it would be as great a thing for God
to give us Christ, and His satisfaction and righteousness, in reward for our obedience as to give us heaven
immediately; it would be as great a reward, and as great
a testimony of respect for our obedience. And if God
gives as great a thing as salvation for our obedience,
why could He not as well give salvation itself directly?
Then there would have been no need of Christ's righteousness. And, indeed, if God gives us Christ, or an interest in Him, properly as a reward of our obedience,
He really gives us salvation in reward for our obedience,
for the former implies the latter—yea, it implies it as
the greater implies the lesser. So that indeed it exalts
our virtue and obedience more to suppose that God
gives us Christ in reward for that virtue and obedience
than if He should give salvation without Christ.

The thing that Scripture guards and militates
against is our imagining that it is our own goodness,
virtue, or excellence that places us in God's acceptance
and favor. But to suppose that God gives us an interest
in Christ as a reward for our virtue is as great an argument that it places us in God's favor as if He bestowed a
title to eternal life as its direct reward. If God gives us
an interest in Christ as a reward for our obedience, it
will then follow that we are placeded in God's acceptance and favor by our own obedience, antecedent to
our having an interest in Christ. For rewarding anyone's excellence evermore supposes favor and acceptance on the account of that excellence. It is the very
notion of a reward that it is a good thing, bestowed in
testimony of respect and favor for the virtue or excellence rewarded.

So that it is not by virtue of our interest in Christ and His merits that we first come into favor with God, according to this scheme; for we are in God's favor before we have any interest in those merits, in that we have an interest in those merits given as a fruit of God's favor for our own virtue. If our interest in Christ is the fruit of God's favor, then it cannot be the ground of it. If God did not accept us, and had no favor for us resulting from our own excellence, He never would bestow so great a reward upon us as a right in Christ's satisfaction and righteousness. So that such a scheme destroys itself, for it supposes that Christ's satisfaction and righteousness are necessary for us to recommend us to the favor of God; and yet it supposes that we have God's favor and acceptance before we have Christ's satisfaction and righteousness, and have these given as a fruit of God's favor.

Indeed, neither salvation itself nor Christ the Savior is given as a reward for anything in man; they are not given as a reward for faith, nor for anything else of ours. We are not united to Christ as a reward *for* our faith, but have union with him *by* faith only as faith is the very act of uniting or closing on our part.

When a man offers himself to a woman in marriage, he does not give himself to her as a reward for her receiving him in marriage. Her receiving him is not considered as a worthy deed in her for which he rewards her by giving himself to her; but it is by her receiving him that the union is made by which she has him for her husband. Her receiving him constitutes the union itself.

By these things, it appears how contrary to the gospel of Christ their scheme is who say that faith justi-

fies as a principle of obedience, as a leading act of obedience, or (as others say) the sum and comprehension
of all evangelical obedience; for by this the obedience
or virtue that is in faith gives it its justifying influence.
And that is the same thing as to say that we are justified
by our own obedience, virtue, or goodness.

Chapter 4

The Place of Obedience

Having thus considered the evidence of the truth of the doctrine of justification by faith alone, I proceed now to the third thing proposed: to show in what sense the acts of a Christian life, or of evangelical obedience, may be looked upon to be concerned in this matter.

From what has been said already it is manifest that they cannot have any concern in this affair as good works, or by virtue of any moral goodness in them; not as works of the law, or as that moral excellence (or any part of it) which is the fulfillment of that great, universal, and everlasting law or covenant of works which the great Lawgiver has established as the highest and unalterable rule of judgment, which Christ alone answers. Nor do these works do anything towards achieving that goodness.

Since it has been shown out of Scripture that it is only by faith, or by the soul's receiving and being united with the Savior who has wrought our righteousness, that we are justified, it therefore remains that the acts of a Christian life cannot be concerned in this affair any otherwise than as they imply and are the expression of faith, and may be looked upon as so many acts of receiving Christ the Savior. But determining what concerns acts of Christian obedience can have in justification in this respect will depend on resolving another point: whether any other act of faith besides the first act has any concern in our justification, or how far perseverance in faith, or the continued and renewed acts of faith, have influence in this affair. And it seems manifest that justification is by the first act of faith, in some respects, in a peculiar manner, because a sinner is actually and finally justified as soon as he has performed one act of faith; and faith in its first act virtually, at least, depends on God for perseverance, and entitles one to this among other benefits. Yet the perseverance of faith is not excluded in this affair; it is not only certainly connected with justification, but it is not to be excluded from that on which the justification of a sinner has a dependence, or that by which he is justified.

I have shown that the way in which justification has a dependence on faith is that it is the qualification on which the congruity of an interest in the righteousness of Christ depends, or wherein such a fitness consists. But the consideration of the perseverance of faith cannot be excluded out of this congruity or fitness, for it is congruous that he who believes in Christ should have an interest in Christ's righteousness, and so in the eternal benefits purchased by it, because faith is that by which the soul has union or oneness with Christ. And there is a natural congruity in it, that they who are one with Christ should have a joint interest with Him in His eternal benefits; yet this congruity depends on it being an abiding union. As it is needful that the branch should abide in the vine in order to receive the lasting benefits of the root, so it is necessary that the soul should abide in Christ in order to receive those lasting benefits of God's final acceptance and favor. John 15:6–7: "If a man abide not in Me, he is cast forth as a branch. If ye abide in Me, and My words abide in you, ye

shall ask what ye will, and it shall be done unto you."
Verses 9–10: "Continue ye in My love. If ye keep (or
abide in) My commandments, ye shall abide in My love,
even as I have kept My Father's commandments, and
abide in His love."

There is the same reason why it is necessary that the
union with Christ should remain as why it should be
begun, and the same reason why it should continue to
be as why it should once be. If it should be begun without remaining, the beginning would be in vain. In order for the soul to be now in a justified state, and free
from condemnation, it is necessary that it should now
be in Christ, and not merely that it should once have
been in Him. Romans 8:1: "There is therefore now no
condemnation to them which are in Christ Jesus." The
soul is saved in Christ as being now in Him, when the
salvation is bestowed, and not merely as remembering
that it once was in Him. Philippians 3:9: "That I may be
found in Him, not having mine own righteousness,
which is of the law, but that which is through the faith
of Christ, the righteousness which is of God by faith."
1 John 2:28: "And now, little children, abide in Him,
that, when He shall appear, we may have confidence,
and not be ashamed before Him at His coming."

In order for persons to be blessed after death, it is
necessary not only that they should once be in Him,
but that they should die in Him. Revelation 14:13:
"Blessed are the dead which die in the Lord." And there
is the same reason why faith, the uniting qualification,
should remain in order for the union to remain; as
there is reason why it should once be in order for the
union to exist in the first place.

So although the sinner is actually and finally justi-

fied on the first acts of faith, yet the perseverance of
faith even then comes into consideration as one thing
on which the fitness of acceptance to life depends.
God, in the act of justification which is passed on a
sinner's first believing, has respect to the perseverance,
as being virtually contained in that first act of faith;
and it is looked upon, and taken by Him who justifies,
as being, as it were, a property in that faith. God has respect to the believer's continuance in faith, and he is
justified by that, as though it already were, because by
divine establishment it shall follow; and it being by divine constitution connected with that first faith, as
much as if it were a property in it, it is then considered
as such, and so justification is not suspended. But were
it not for this, it would be needful that it should be suspended until the sinner had actually persevered in
faith.

And that it is so, that God in the act of final justification which He passes at the sinner's conversion has
respect to perseverance in faith and future acts of faith,
as being virtually implied in the first act, is further
manifest by this: that in a sinner's justification, at his
conversion, there is virtually contained a forgiveness as
to eternal and deserved punishment not only of all past
sins, but also of all future infirmities and acts of sin
that the sinner shall be guilty of. And this is because
that first justification is decisive and final. And yet pardon, in the order of nature, properly follows the crime,
and also follows those acts of repentance and faith that
respect the crime pardoned, as is manifest from both
reason and Scripture.

David, in the beginning of Psalm 32, speaks of the
forgiveness of sins (which were doubtless committed

long after he was first godly) as if it followed those sins, and on his repentance and faith with respect to them. And yet this forgiveness is spoken of by the apostle in Romans 4 as an instance of justification by faith. Probably the sin David there speaks of is the same that he committed in the matter of Uriah, and so the pardon is the same as the release from death or eternal punishment of which the prophet Nathan speaks in 2 Samuel 12:13: "The Lord also hath put away thy sin; thou shalt not die." Not only does the manifestation of this pardon follow the sin in the order of time, but the pardon itself, in the order of nature, follows David's repentance and faith with respect to this sin; for it is spoken of in Psalm 32 as depending on it.

But inasmuch as a sinner, in his first justification, is forever justified and freed from all obligation to eternal punishment, it hence, of necessity, follows that future faith and repentance are beheld in that justification as virtually contained in that first faith and repentance because repentance of those future sins, and faith in a Redeemer, with respect to them—or at least the continuance of that habit and principle in the heart that has such an actual repentance and faith in its nature and tendency—is now made sure by God's promise. If remission of sins committed after conversion, in the order of nature, follows that faith and repentance which is after them, then it follows that future sins are respected in the first justification in no other way than as future faith and repentance are respected in it. And future repentance and faith are looked upon by Him who justifies as virtually implied in the first repentance and faith in the same manner as justification from future sins is virtually implied in the first justification, which is the thing that was to be proved.

And besides, if no other act of faith could be concerned in justification but the first act, it would then follow that Christians ought never to seek justification by any other act of faith. For if justification is not to be obtained by later acts of faith, then surely it is not a duty to seek it by such acts; and so it can never be a duty for persons, once they are converted, by faith to seek God, or believingly to look to Him, for the remission of sin or deliverance from the guilt of it, because deliverance from the guilt of sin is part of what belongs to justification. And if it is not proper for converts to look by faith to God through Christ for it, then it will follow that it is not proper for them to pray for it; for Christian prayer to God for a blessing is but an expression of faith in God for that blessing. Prayer is only the voice of faith. But if these things are so, it will follow that the petition in the Lord's prayer, "forgive us our debts," is not proper to be put up by disciples of Christ, or to be used in Christian assemblies, and then Christ improperly directed His disciples to use that petition when they were all, except Judas, converted before.

The debt for which Christ directs His disciples to pray for forgiveness can mean nothing else but the punishment that sin deserves, or the debt that we owe to divine justice, the ten thousand talents we owe our Lord. To pray that God would forgive our debts is undoubtedly the same thing as to pray that God would release us from obligation to due punishment; but releasing us from obligation to the punishment due to sin, and forgiving the debt that we owe to divine justice, is what pertains to justification.

And to suppose that no later acts of faith are concerned in the business of justification, so that it is not proper for anyone ever to seek justification by such acts, would be forever to cut off those Christians who are doubtful concerning their first act of faith from the joy and peace of believing. As the business of a justifying faith is to obtain pardon and peace with God by looking to God and trusting in Him for these blessings, so the joy and peace of that faith is in the apprehension of pardon and peace obtained by such a trust. A Christian who is doubtful of his first act of faith cannot have this from that act because, by the supposition, he is doubtful whether it is an act of faith, and so whether he obtained pardon and peace by that act.

The proper remedy in such a case is now by faith to look to God in Christ for these blessings; but he is cut off from this remedy because he is uncertain whether he has warrant so to do. For he does not know but that he has believed already, and, if so, then he has no warrant to look to God by faith for these blessings now because, by the supposition, no new act of faith is a proper means of obtaining these blessings. And so he can never properly obtain the joy of faith; for there are acts of true faith that are very weak, and the first act may be so as well as others. It may be like the first motion of the infant in the womb; it may be so weak an act that the Christian, by examining it, may never be able to determine whether it was a true act of faith or not. And it is evident from fact and abundant experience that many Christians are forever at a loss to determine which was their first act of faith. And those saints who have had a good degree of satisfaction concerning their faith may be subject to great declensions and falls, in which case they are liable to great fears of eternal punishment; and the proper way of deliverance is to forsake their sin by repentance, and by faith now to come to Christ for deliverance from the deserved eternal punishment. But this would not be true if deliverance from that punishment could not be obtained in this way.

But what is still a more plain and direct evidence of what I am now arguing for is that the act of faith which Abraham exercised in the great promise of the covenant of grace that God made to him (of which it is expressly said in Galatians 3:6, "It was accounted to him for righteousness"), the grand instance and proof that the apostle so much insists upon throughout Romans 4 and Galatians 3 to confirm his doctrine of justification by faith alone, was not Abraham's first act of faith, but was exerted long after he had by faith forsaken his own country (Hebrews 11:8), and had been treated as an eminent friend of God.

Moreover, the Apostle Paul, in Philippians 3, tells us how earnestly he sought justification by faith, or to win Christ and obtain that righteousness which was by the faith of Him, in what he did after his conversion. Verses 8–9: "For whom I have suffered the loss of all things, and do count them but dung that I may win Christ, and be found in Him, not having mine own righteousness which is of the law, but that which is through the faith of Christ, the righteousness which is of God by faith." And in the next two verses he expresses the same thing in other words, and tells us how he went through sufferings, and became conformable to Christ's death, that he might be a partaker with Christ in the benefit of His resurrection, which the same apostle elsewhere teaches us is especially justifica-

tion. Christ's resurrection was His justification in this:
He who was put to death in the flesh was justified by the
Spirit, and He who was delivered for our offenses rose
again for our justification. And the apostle tells us in
the verses that follow in that third chapter of Philippians that he thus sought to attain the righteousness
which is through the faith of Christ, and so to partake
of the benefit of His resurrection, still as though he
had not already attained, but that he continued to follow after it.

On the whole, it appears that the perseverance of
faith is necessary even to the congruity of justification;
and that no less because a sinner is justified and perseverance is promised on the first act of faith, but because
God in that justification has respect not only to the past
act of faith, but to His own promise of future acts, and
to the fitness of a qualification beheld as yet only in His
own promise. Perseverance in faith is thus necessary to
salvation not merely as a *sine qua non,* or as an universal
concomitant of it, but by reason of such an influence
and dependence. This seems manifest by many Scriptures. Hebrews 3:6: "Whose house are we, if we hold fast
the confidence, and the rejoicing of the hope firm
unto the end." Verse 14: "For we are made partakers of
Christ, if we hold the beginning of our confidence
steadfast unto the end." Hebrews 6:12: "Be ye followers
of them who through faith and patience inherit the
promises." Romans 11:20: "Well, because of unbelief
they were broken off; but thou standest by faith. Be not
high-minded, but fear."

And as the congruity of a final justification depends
on perseverance in faith as well as the first act, so often-
times the manifestation of justification in the con-

science arises a great deal more from later acts than
from the first act. And all the difference whereby the
first act of faith has a concern in this affair that is peculiar seems to be, as it were, only an accidental difference arising from the circumstance of time, or its being first in order of time, and not from any peculiar respect that God has for it, or any influence it has of a peculiar nature in the affair of our salvation.

And thus it is that a truly Christian walk and the acts
of an evangelical, childlike, believing obedience are
concerned in the affair of our justification, and seem to
be sometimes so spoken of in Scripture, that is, as an
expression of a persevering faith in the Son of God, the
only Savior.

Faith unites to Christ, and so gives a congruity to
justification not merely as remaining a dormant principle in the heart, but as being and appearing in its active expressions. The obedience of a Christian, so far as
it is truly evangelical and performed with the Spirit of
the Son sent forth into the heart, has all relation to
Christ, the Mediator, and is but an expression of the
soul's believing union with Christ. All evangelical
works are works of that faith which works by love; and
every such act of obedience, wherein it is inward and
the act of the soul, is only a new, effective act of reception of Christ, and adherence to the glorious Savior.
Hence we have the words of the apostle in Galatians
2:20: "I live; yet not I, but Christ liveth in me; and the
life that I now live in the flesh I live by the faith of the
Son of God." And hence we are directed, in whatever we
do, whether in word or deed, to do all in the name of
the Lord Jesus Christ (Colossians 3:17).

That God in justification has respect not only to the

first act of faith, but also to future persevering acts as expressed in life, seems manifest by Romans 1:17: "For therein is the righteousness of God revealed from faith to faith; as it is written, 'The just shall live by faith.' " And Hebrews 10:38–39: "Now the just shall live by faith; but if any man draw back, My soul shall have no pleasure in him. But we are not of them who draw back unto perdition, but of them that believe, to the saving of the soul."

So that as was before said of faith, so may it be said of a childlike, believing obedience: it has no concern in justification by any virtue or excellence in it, but only as there is a reception of Christ in it. And this is no more contrary to the apostle's frequent assertion of our being justified without the works of the law than to say that we are justified by faith; for faith is as much a work or act of Christian obedience as the expressions of faith are in spiritual life and walk. And therefore, as we say that faith does not justify as a work, so we say of all these effective expressions of faith.

This is the reverse of the scheme of our modern divines who hold that faith justifies only as an act or expression of obedience, whereas in truth obedience has no concern in justification in any other way than as an expression of faith.

Chapter 5

Objections Answered

OBJECTION 1. We frequently find promises of eternal life and salvation, and sometimes of justification itself, made to our own virtue and obedience. Eternal life is promised to obedience in Romans 2:7: "To them, who by patient continuance in well-doing seek for glory, honor, and immortality, eternal life." The like is given in innumerable other places. And justification itself is promised to that virtue of a forgiving spirit or temper in us in Matthew 6:14: "For if ye forgive men their trespasses, your heavenly Father will also forgive you; but if ye forgive not men their trespasses, neither will your Father forgive your trespasses." All allow that justification in great part consists in the forgiveness of sins.

ANSWER 1. These things being promised to our virtue and obedience argue no more than that there is a connection between them and evangelical obedience, which, as I have already observed, is not in dispute. All that can be proven by obedience and salvation being connected in the promise is that obedience and salvation are connected in fact, which nobody denies. And whether it is owned or denied is, as has been shown, irrelevant to our purpose. There is no need that an admission to a title to salvation should be given on the account of our obedience in order for the promises to be true. If we find such a promise, that he who obeys shall be saved, or he who is holy shall be justified, all that is needful in order for such promises to be true is that it is really so that he who obeys shall be saved, and that holiness and justification shall indeed go together. That proposition may be true, that he who obeys shall be saved, because obedience and salvation are connected together in fact, and yet an acceptance to a title to salvation may not be granted upon the account of any of our own virtue or obedience. What is a promise but a declaration of future truth for the comfort and encouragement of the person to whom it is declared? Promises are conditional propositions, and, as has been already observed, it is not in dispute whether other things besides faith may have the place of the condition in such propositions wherein pardon and salvation are the consequence.

ANSWER 2. Promises may rationally be made to signs and evidences of faith, and yet the thing promised may not be upon the account of the sign itself, but the thing signified. Thus, for instance, human government may rationally make promises of such and such privileges to those who can show such evidences of their being free of such a city, or members of such a corporation, or descended from such a family, when it is not at all for the sake of that which is the evidence or sign (in itself considered) that they are admitted to such a privilege, but only and purely for the sake of that of which it is an evidence. And though God does not stand in need of signs to know whether we have true faith or not, yet our own consciences do—so that it is much for our comfort that promises are made to signs of faith. Finding in ourselves a forgiving temper and disposition may be a most proper and natural evidence

to our consciences that our hearts have, in a sense of
our own utter unworthiness, truly closed and fallen in
with the way of free and infinitely gracious forgiveness
of our sins by Jesus Christ; whence we may be enabled,
with the greater comfort, to apply to ourselves the
promises of forgiveness by Christ.

ANSWER 3. It has been just now shown how acts of
evangelical obedience are indeed concerned in our justification itself, and are not excluded from that condition that justification depends upon, without the least
prejudice to that doctrine of justification by faith, without any goodness of our own, that has been maintained. And therefore it can be no objection against
this doctrine that we have sometimes in Scripture
promises of pardon and acceptance made to such acts
of obedience.

ANSWER 4. Promises of particular benefits implied
in justification and salvation may especially be fitly
made to such expressions and evidences of faith as they
have a peculiar natural likeness and suitableness to. As
forgiveness is promised to a forgiving spirit in us, obtaining mercy is fitly promised to mercifulness in us,
and the like, and that upon several accounts. These are
the most natural evidences of our heart's closing with
those benefits by faith, for they especially show the
sweet accord and consent that exist between the heart
and these benefits. And by reason of the natural likeness there is between the virtue and the benefit, the
one has the greater tendency to bring the other to
mind. The practice of the virtue tends the more to re-
new the sense and refresh the hope of the blessing
promised, and also to convince the conscience of the
justice of being denied the benefit if the duty is

neglected. Besides, the sense and manifestation of divine forgiveness in our own consciences—yea, and
many exercises of God's forgiving mercy (as it respects
God's fatherly displeasures) granted after justification
through the course of a Christian life—may be given as
the proper rewards for a forgiving spirit, and yet this is
not at all to the prejudice of the doctrine we have maintained. This will more fully appear when we come to
answer the next objection.

OBJECTION 2. Our own obedience and inherent
holiness are necessary to prepare men for heaven; and
therefore they are, doubtless, what recommends persons to God's acceptance as the heirs of heaven.
To this I answer:
1. Our own obedience being necessary in order to
prepare for an actual bestowment of glory is no argument that it is the thing upon account of which we are
accepted to a right to it. God may and does do many
things to prepare the saints for glory after He has accepted them as the heirs of glory. A parent may do
much to prepare a child for an inheritance in its education after the child is an heir; yea, there are many
things necessary to fit a child for the actual possession
of the inheritance, yet not necessary for the child to
have a right to the inheritance.
2. If everything that is necessary to prepare men for
glory must be the proper condition of justification,
then perfect holiness is the condition of justification.
Men must be made perfectly holy before they are admitted to the enjoyment of the blessedness of heaven; for
there must in no way enter in there any spiritual de-
filement. And therefore, when a saint dies, he leaves all

his sin and corruption when he leaves the body.

OBJECTION 3. Our obedience is not only indissolubly connected with salvation and preparatory to it, but the Scripture expressly speaks of bestowing eternal blessings as rewards for the good deeds of the saints. Matthew 10:42: "Whosoever shall give to drink unto one of these little ones a cup of cold water only, in the name of a disciple, he shall in no wise lose his reward." 1 Corinthians 3:8: "Every man shall receive his own reward, according to his own labor." There are many other places.

This seems to militate against the doctrine that has been maintained in two ways:

1. Bestowing a reward carries in it a respect to a moral fitness in the thing rewarded for its reward, since the very notion of a reward is a benefit bestowed in testimony of acceptance of and respect to the goodness or amiableness of some qualification or work in the person rewarded. Besides, the Scripture seems to explain itself in this matter in Revelation 3:4: "Thou hast a few names, even in Sardis, which have not defiled their garments; and they shall walk with Me in white, for they are worthy." This is given as the reason why they should have such a reward: because they were worthy. Though we suppose this to imply no proper merit, yet it as least implies a moral fitness, or that the excellence of their virtue in God's sight recommends them to such a reward—which seems directly repugnant to what has been supposed, which is that we are accepted and approved by God as the heirs of salvation not out of regard to the excellence of our own virtue or goodness, or any moral fitness therein for such a reward, but only on

account of the dignity and moral fitness of Christ's righteousness.

2. Our being eternally rewarded for our own holiness and good works necessarily supposes that our future happiness will be greater or smaller in some proportion as our own holiness and obedience are greater or lesser. And that there are different degrees of glory, according to different degrees of virtue and good works, is a doctrine very expressly and frequently taught us in Scripture. But this seems quite inconsistent with the saints all having their future blessedness as a reward of Christ's righteousness; for if Christ's righteousness is imputed to all, and this is what entitles each one to glory, then it is the same righteousness that entitles one to glory which entitles another. But if all have glory as the reward of the same righteousness, why have not all the same glory? Does not the same righteousness merit as much glory when imputed to one as when imputed to another?

In answer to the first part of this objection, I would observe that it does not argue that we are justified by our good deeds if we say we shall have eternal blessings in reward for them; for it is in consequence of our justification that our good deeds become rewardable with spiritual and eternal rewards. The acceptableness, and so the rewardableness, of our virtue are not antecedent to justification, but follow it, and are built entirely upon it. This is the reverse of what those in the adverse scheme of justification suppose, which is that justification is built on the acceptableness and rewardablenss of our virtue. They suppose that a saving interest in Christ is given as a reward for our virtue, or (which is the same thing) as a testimony of God's acceptance of our excellence in our virtue. But the contrary is true: God's respect for our virtue as our amiableness in His sight, and His acceptance of it as rewardable, are entirely built on our interest in Christ being already established. So that the relation to Christ whereby believers, in Scripture language, are said to be in Christ is the very foundation of our virtues and good deeds being accepted by God, and so their being rewarded; for a reward is a testimony of acceptance. For we, and all that we do, are accepted only in the Beloved (Ephesians 1:6).

Our sacrifices are acceptable only through our interest in Him, and through His worthiness and preciousness being, as it were, made ours. 1 Peter 2:4–5: "To whom coming, as unto a living stone, disallowed indeed of men, but chosen of God, and precious, ye also, as lively stones, are built up as a spiritual house, an holy priesthood, to offer up spiritual sacrifices, acceptable to God by Jesus Christ." Here being actually built on this stone which is precious to God is mentioned as all the ground of the acceptance of our good works to God, and their becoming also precious in his eyes. So Hebrews 13:21: "May the God of peace make you perfect in every good work to do His will, working in you that which is well-pleasing in His sight, through Jesus Christ." And hence we are directed, whatever we offer to God, to offer it in Christ's name, expecting to have it accepted in no other way than from the value that God places on that name. Colossians 3:17: "And whatsoever ye do, in word or deed, do all in the name of the Lord Jesus, giving thanks to God and the Father by Him." To act in Christ's name is to act under Him as our Head, and as having Him to stand for us and represent us toward God.

The reason for this may be seen from what has already been said, to show it is not fitting that anything in us should be accepted by God as any excellence of our persons until we are actually in Christ and justified through Him. The loveliness of the virtue of fallen creatures is nothing in the sight of God till He beholds them in Christ, clothed with His righteousness:

• Because till then we stand condemned before God by His own holy law, to His utter rejection and abhorrence.

• Because we are infinitely guilty before Him, and the loveliness of our virtue bears no proportion to our guilt, and must therefore pass for nothing before a strict judge.

• Because our good deeds and virtuous acts themselves are in a sense corrupt, and the hatefulness of the corruption of them, if we are beheld as we are in ourselves or separate from Christ, infinitely outweighs the loveliness of the good that is in them. So that if no other sin is considered but that which attends the act of virtue itself, the loveliness vanishes into nothing in comparison to it. And therefore the virtue must pass for nothing, outside of Christ.

Not only are our best duties defiled—in being attended with the exercises of sin and corruption which precede, follow, and are intermingled with them—but even the holy acts themselves, and the gracious exercises of the godly, are defective. Though the act most simply considered is good, yet take the acts in their measure and dimensions, and the manner in which they are exerted, and they are sinfully defective. There is that defect in them that may well be called the corruption of them. That defect is properly sin, an expression

of a vile sinfulness of heart, and what tends to provoke
the just anger of God—not because the exercise of love
and other grace is not equal to God's loveliness (for it
is impossible that the love of creatures, whether men
and angels, should be so), but because the act is so very
disproportionate to the occasion given for love or other
grace, considering God's loveliness, the manifestation
that is made of it, the exercises of kindness, the capacity of human nature, and our advantages (and the like)
together.

A negative expression of corruption may be as truly
sin, and as just cause of provocation, as a positive. Thus,
if a worthy and excellent person should, from mere
generosity and goodness, exceedingly lay out himself,
and with great expense and suffering save another's
life, or redeem him from some extreme calamity, and if
that other person should never thank him for it, or express the least gratitude in any way, this would be a
negative expression of his ingratitude and baseness.
But it is equivalent to an act of ingratitude, or a positive
exercise of a base unworthy spirit, and is truly an expression of it, and brings as much blame as if he, by
some positive act, had greatly injured another person.
And so it would be (only in a lesser degree) if the gratitude was but very small, bearing no proportion to the
benefit and obligation; as if, for so great and extraordi-
nary a kindness, he should express no more gratitude
than would have been becoming towards a person who
had only given him a cup of water when thirsty, shown
him the way in a journey when lost, or done him some
such small kindness. If he should come to his benefac-
tor to express his gratitude, and should behave after
this manner, he might truly be said to act unworthily

and odiously; he would show a most ungrateful spirit. His behaving in such a manner might justly be abhorred by all; and yet the gratitude, what little there is of it, most simply considered, and so far as it goes, is good.

And so it is with respect to our exercise of love, gratitude, and other graces, towards God. They are defectively corrupt and sinful, and, taking them as they are in their manner and measure, might justly be odious and provoking to God, and would necessarily be so were we beheld outside of Christ. For in that this defect is sin, it is infinitely hateful; and so the hatefulness of the very act infinitely outweighs the loveliness of it, because all sin has infinite hatefulness and heinousness. But our holiness has but little value and loveliness, as has been elsewhere demonstrated.

Hence, though it is true that the saints are rewarded for their good works, yet it is for Christ's sake only, and not for the excellence of their works in themselves considered, or beheld separately from Christ; for so they have no excellence in God's sight, or acceptableness to Him, as has now been shown. It is acknowledged that God, in rewarding the holiness and good works of believers, does in some respect give them happiness as a testimony of His respect for the loveliness of their holiness and good works in His sight; for that is the very notion of a reward. But it is in a very different sense from what would have been if man had not fallen—which would have been to bestow eternal life on man as a testimony of God's respect for the loveliness of what man did, considered as in itself, and as in man separately by himself, and not beheld as a member of Christ. In this sense also, the scheme of justification we are opposing necessarily supposes that the excellence of our virtue should be respected and rewarded; for it supposes a saving interest in Christ itself to be given as its reward.

Two things come to pass relating to the saints' reward for their inherent righteousness by virtue of their relation to Christ:

First, the guilt of their persons is all done away with, and the pollution and hatefulness that attends and is in their good works is hidden.

Second, their relation to Christ adds a positive value and dignity to their good works in God's sight. That little holiness, and those faint and feeble acts of love and other graces, receive an exceeding value in the sight of God by virtue of God's beholding them as in Christ, and, as it were, members of one so infinitely worthy in His eyes. That is because God looks upon these persons as of greater dignity on this account. Isaiah 43:4: "Since thou wast precious in My sight, thou hast been honorable." God, for Christ's sake, and because they are members of His own righteous and dear Son, sets an exceeding value upon their persons. And hence it follows that He also gets a great value upon their good acts and offerings.

The same love and obedience in a person of greater dignity and value in God's sight is more valuable in His eyes than in one of less dignity. Love is valuable in proportion to the dignity of the person whose love it is, because, so far as anyone gives his love to another, he gives himself, in that he gives his heart. But this is a more excellent offering in proportion as the person whose self is offered is more worthy. Believers become immensely more honorable in God's esteem by virtue of their relation to Christ than man would have been considered by himself, even if he were free from sin. A lowly person becomes more honorable when married to a king. Hence God will probably reward the little, weak love and poor, exceedingly imperfect obedience of believers in Christ with more glorious reward than He would have done Adam's perfect obedience. According to the tenor of the first covenant, the person was to be accepted and rewarded only for the work's sake; but by the covenant of grace the work is accepted and rewarded only for the person's sake, the person being beheld antecedently as a member of Christ, and clothed with His righteousness.

So that though the saints' inherent holiness is rewarded, yet this very reward is indeed no less founded on the worthiness and righteousness of Christ. None of the value that their works have in His sight, nor any of the acceptance they have with Him, is outside of Christ and outside of His righteousness. But His worthiness as Mediator is the prime and only foundation on which all is built, and the universal source from whence all arises. God indeed does great things out of regard to the saints' loveliness, but it is only as a secondary and derivative loveliness. When I speak of a derivative loveliness, I do not mean only that the qualifications themselves accepted as lovely are derived from Christ, and from His power and purchase, but that the acceptance of them as a loveliness, and all the value that is set upon them, and all their connection with the reward, is founded in and derived from Christ's righteousness and worthiness.

If we suppose that not only higher degrees of glory in heaven, but heaven itself is in some respect given in reward for the holiness and good works of the saints in this secondary and derivative sense, it will not prejudice the doctrine we have maintained. It is in no way impossible that God may bestow heaven's glory wholly out of respect to Christ's righteousness, and yet in reward for man's inherent holiness, in different respects and different ways. It may be only Christ's righteousness that God respects for its own sake, the independent acceptableness and dignity of it being sufficient of itself to recommend all who believe in Christ to a title to this glory; and so it may be only by this that persons enter into a title to heaven, or have their prime right to it. And yet God may also have respect for the saints' own holiness for Christ's sake, and as deriving a value from Christ's merit, to which He may testify in bestowing heaven upon them. The saints being beheld as members of Christ, their obedience is looked upon by God as something of Christ's, it being the obedience of the members of Christ, just as the sufferings of the members of Christ are looked upon, in some respect, as the sufferings of Christ. Hence the apostle, speaking of his sufferings, says in Colossians 1:24: "Who now rejoice in my sufferings for you, and fill up that which is behind of the afflictions of Christ in my flesh." To the same purpose is Matthew 25:35: "I was an hungered, naked, sick, and in prison . . . ." And Revelation 11:8: "And their dead bodies shall lie in the street of the great city, which spiritually is called Sodom and Egypt, where also our Lord was crucified."

By the merit and righteousness of Christ, such favor of God towards the believer may be obtained as that God may hereby be already, as it were, disposed to make them perfectly and eternally happy. But yet this does

not hinder God in His wisdom from choosing to bestow this perfect and eternal happiness in this way, that
is, in some respect as a reward for their holiness and
obedience. It is not impossible that the blessedness
may be bestowed as a reward for that which is done after an interest is already obtained in that favor which
(to speak of God after the manner of men) disposes
God to bestow the blessedness. Our heavenly Father
may already have that favor for a child whereby He may
be thoroughly ready to give the child an inheritance
because he is His child, which he is by the purchase of
Christ's righteousness; and yet the Father may choose
to bestow the inheritance on the child in a way of reward for his dutifulness, and behaving in a manner becoming a child. And so great a reward may be judged to
be not more than a fitting reward for his dutifulness.
But that so great a reward is judged fitting does not
arise from the excellence of the obedience absolutely
considered, but from his standing in so near and honorable a relation to God as that of a child, which is obtained only by the righteousness of Christ.

And thus the reward, and the greatness of it, arises
properly from the righteousness of Christ, though it is
indeed in some sort the reward for their obedience. A
father might justly esteem the inheritance to be no
more than a fitting reward for the obedience of his
child, and yet esteem it more than a meet reward for
the obedience of a servant. The favor whence a believer's heavenly Father bestows the eternal inheritance
and his title as an heir is founded in that relation he
stands in to Him as a child, purchased by Christ's righteousness, even though He in wisdom chooses to bestow it in such a way as therein to testify to His accep-

tance of the amiableness of his obedience in Christ.

Believers having a title to heaven by faith antecedent to their obedience, or its being absolutely promised to them before, does not hinder that the actual bestowal of heaven may also be a testimony of God's regard for their obedience, though performed afterwards. Thus it was with Abraham, the father and pattern of all believers: God bestowed upon him that blessing of multiplying his seed as the stars of heaven, and causing that in his seed all the families of the earth should be blessed, in reward for his obedience in offering up his son Isaac. Genesis 22:16–18: "And the angel said, 'By myself have I sworn,' saith the LORD, 'because thou hast done this thing, and hast not withheld thy son, thine only son, that in blessing I will bless thee, and in multiplying I will multiply thy seed as the stars of the heaven, and as the sand which is upon the sea shore; and thy seed shall possess the gate of his enemies, and in thy seed shall all the nations of the earth be blessed, because thou hast obeyed My voice.' " And yet the very same blessings had been from time to time promised to Abraham, in the most positive terms, and the promise, with great solemnity, confirmed and sealed to him (Genesis 12:2–3; 13:16; 15:1–7; chapter 17; 18:10, 18).

From what has been said we may easily solve the difficulty arising from that text in Revelation 3:4: "They shall walk with me in white, for they are worthy," which is parallel with that text in Luke 20:35: "But they which shall be accounted worthy to obtain that world, and the resurrection from the dead." I allow (as in the objection) that this worthiness doubtless denotes a moral fitness for the reward, or that God looks on these glori-

ous benefits as a fitting testimony of His regard for the
value which their persons and performances have in
His sight.

God looks on these glorious benefits as a meet testimony of his regard for the value which their persons
have in His sight. But He sets this value upon their persons purely for Christ's sake. They are such jewels, and
have such preciousness in His eyes, only because they
are beheld in Christ, and by reason of the worthiness of
the Head they are the members of, and the stock they
are grafted into. And the value that God sets upon them
on this account is so great that God thinks it fitting,
out of regard for it, to admit them to such exceeding
glory. The saints, on account of their relation to Christ,
are such precious jewels in God's sight that they are
thought worthy of a place in His own crown (Malachi
3:17; Zechariah 9:16). So far as the saints are said to be
valuable in God's sight, on whatever account, so far
may they properly be said to be worthy or meet for that
honor which is answerable to the value or price which
God sets upon them. A child or wife of a prince is worthy to be treated with great honor; and therefore, if a
lowly person should be adopted as a child of a prince,
or should be espoused to a prince, it would be proper to
say that she was worthy of such and such honor and respect; and there would be no misuse of the words in
saying that she ought to have such respect paid her for
she is worthy, though it is only on account of her relation to the prince that she is so.

From the value God sets upon their persons for the
sake of Christ's worthiness, He also sets a high value on
their virtue and performances. Their meek and quiet
spirit is of great price in His sight. Their fruits are

pleasant fruits; their offerings are an odor of sweet
smell to Him, and that because of the value He sets on
their persons, as has been already observed and explained. This preciousness or high valuableness of believers is a moral fitness for a reward, and yet this valuableness is all in the righteousness of Christ; that is the
foundation of it. The thing respected is not excellence
in them separately by themselves, or their virtue by itself, but the value in God's account arises from other
considerations. This is the natural import of Luke 20:35
("they which shall be accounted worthy to obtain that
world") and Luke 21:36 ("that ye may be accounted worthy to escape all these things that shall come to pass,
and to stand before the Son of man"). 2 Thessalonians
1:5: "That ye may be counted worthy of the kingdom of
God, for which ye also suffer."

There is a vast difference between this scheme and
what is supposed in the scheme of those who oppose
the doctrine of justification by faith alone. This lays the
foundation of first acceptance with God, and all actual
salvation consequent upon it, wholly in Christ and His
righteousness. On the contrary, in their scheme a regard for man's own excellence or virtue is supposed to
come first, and to have the place of the first foundation
in actual salvation, though not in that ineffectual redemption which they suppose is common to all. They
lay the foundation of all discriminating salvation in
man's own virtue and moral excellence. This is the very
bottom stone in this affair; for they suppose that it is
from regard for our virtue that even a special interest in
Christ itself is given. The foundation being so contrary,
the whole scheme becomes exceedingly diverse and
contrary; the one is an evangelical scheme, the other a

legal one; the one is utterly inconsistent with our being justified by Christ's righteousness, the other not at all.

From what has been said, we may understand not only how the forgiveness of sin granted in justification is indissolubly connected with a forgiving spirit in us, but how there may be many exercises of forgiving mercy granted in reward for our forgiving those who trespass against us. For none will deny that there are many acts of divine forgiveness towards the saints that do not presuppose an unjustified state immediately preceding that forgiveness. None will deny that saints who never fell from a justified state yet commit many sins which God forgives afterwards by laying aside His fatherly displeasure. This forgiveness may be in reward for our forgiveness without any prejudice to the doctrine that has been maintained, as well as other mercies and blessings consequent on justification.

With respect to the second part of the objection, that relates to the different degrees of glory and the seeming inconsistency there is in considering that the degrees of glory in different saints should be greater or lesser according to their inherent holiness and good works, and yet that everyone's glory should be purchased with the price of the very same imputed righteousness, I answer that Christ, by His righteousness, purchased for everyone complete and perfect happiness according to his capacity. But this does not hinder that the saints, being of various capacities, may have various degrees of happiness, and yet all their happiness is the fruit of Christ's purchase. Indeed, it cannot be properly said that Christ purchased any particular degree of happiness, so that the value of Christ's righteousness in the sight of God is sufficient to raise a believer so high in happiness and no higher, or so that if the believer were made happier it would exceed the value of Christ's righteousness; but in general, Christ purchased eternal life, or perfect happiness for all, according to their various capacities.

The saints are as so many vessels of different sizes, cast into a sea of happiness, where every vessel is full; this Christ purchased for all. But after all, it is left to God's sovereign pleasure to determine the largeness of the vessel. Christ's righteousness does not meddle with this matter. Ephesians 4:4–5, 7: "There is one body, and one Spirit, even as ye are called in one hope of your calling; one Lord, one faith, one baptism. . . . But unto every one of us is given grace according to the measure of the gift of Christ." God may dispense in this matter according to what rule He pleases, no less for what Christ has done. He may dispense either without condition, or upon what condition He pleases to fix.

It is evident that Christ's righteousness does not meddle with this matter; for what Christ did was to fulfill the covenant of works, but the covenant of works did not meddle at all with this. If Adam had persevered in perfect obedience, he and his posterity would have had perfect and full happiness. Everyone's happiness would have so answered his capacity that he would have been completely blessed; but God would have been at liberty to have made some of one capacity and others of another, as He pleased. The angels have obtained eternal life, or a state of confirmed glory, by a covenant of works, whose condition was perfect obedience; yet some are higher in glory than others, according to the various capacities that God, according to His sovereign pleasure, has given them. So that since it is still left

with God, notwithstanding the perfect obedience of the
second Adam, to fix the degree of each one's capacity
by what rule He pleases, He has been pleased to fix the
degree of capacity, and so of glory, by the proportion of
the saints' grace and fruitfulness here. He gives higher
degrees of glory as reward for higher degrees of holiness and good works because it pleases Him; and yet all
the happiness of each saint is indeed the fruit of the
purchase of Christ's obedience. If it had been but one
man for whom Christ had obeyed and died, and it had
pleased God to make him of a very large capacity,
Christ's perfect obedience would have purchased that
his capacity should be filled, and then all his happiness
might properly be said to be the fruit of Christ's perfect
obedience—though, if he had been of a lesser capacity,
he would not have had so much happiness by the same
obedience, and yet would have had as much as Christ
merited for him. Christ's righteousness does not meddle with the degree of happiness in any other way than
as He merits that it should be full and perfect according to the capacity. And so it may be said to be concerned in the degree of happiness, as perfect is a degree with respect to imperfect; but it meddles not with
degrees of perfect happiness.

This matter may be yet better understood if we consider that Christ and the whole church of saints are, as
it were, one body, of which He is the Head and they are
members of different place and capacity. Now the
whole body—Head and members—have communion in
Christ's righteousness; they are all partakers of the
benefit of it. Christ Himself, the Head, is rewarded for
it, and every member is partaker of the benefit and reward. But it by no means follows that every part should

equally partake of the benefit, but every part in proportion to its place and capacity. The Head partakes of far more than other parts, and the more noble members partake of more than do the inferior ones. In a natural body that enjoys perfect health, the head, heart, and lungs have a greater share of this health; they have it more seated in them than the hands and feet because they are parts of greater capacity, though the hands and feet are as much in perfect health as those nobler parts of the body. So it is in the mystical body of Christ: all the members are partakers of the benefit of the Head, but it is according to the different capacity and place they have in the body. And God determines that place and capacity as He pleases. He makes whom He pleases the foot, whom He pleases the hand, and whom he pleases the lungs. 1 Corinthians 12:18: "God set the members every one of them in the body, as it hath pleased Him." God efficaciously determines the place and capacity of every member by the different degrees of grace (and assistance in the improvement of that grace) in this world. Those whom He intends for the highest place in the body, He gives them most of His Spirit, the greatest share of the divine nature, the Spirit and nature of Christ Jesus the Head, and that assistance whereby they perform the most excellent works and most abound in them.

OBJECTION 4. It may be objected against what has been supposed (that rewards are given for our good works only in consequence of an interest in Christ, or in testimony of God's respect for the excellence or value of them in His sight, as built on an interest in Christ's righteousness already obtained) that the

Scripture speaks of an interest in Christ itself as being given out of respect for our moral fitness. Matthew 10:37–39: "He that loveth father or mother more than Me is not worthy of Me; he that loveth son or daughter more than Me is not worthy of Me. And he that taketh not his cross and followeth after Me is not worthy of Me. He that findeth his life shall lose it." Worthiness here at least signifies a moral fitness, or an excellence that recommends. And this passage seems to intimate that it is out of respect for a moral fitness that men are admitted to a union with Christ and an interest in Him. And therefore this worthiness cannot be consequent on being in Christ and by the imputation of His worthiness, or from any value that is in us or in our actions in God's sight, as beheld in Christ.

To this I answer that, though persons, when they are accepted, are not accepted as worthy, yet when they are rejected they are rejected as unworthy. He who does not love Christ above other things, but treats Him with such indignity as to set Him below earthly things, shall be treated as unworthy of Christ. His unworthiness of Christ, especially in that particular, shall be marked against him and imputed to him. And though he is a professing Christian, lives in the enjoyment of the gospel, and has been visibly engrafted into Christ and admitted as one of His disciples, as Judas was, yet he shall be thrust out in wrath as a punishment for his vile treatment of Christ.

The aforementioned words do not imply that if a man loves Christ above father and mother he would be worthy; the most they imply is that one who does not do this shall be treated and thrust out as unworthy. He who believes is not received for the worthiness or moral fitness of faith; yet the professing but untrue Christian is cast out by God for the unworthiness and moral unfitness of unbelief. Being accepted as one of Christ's is not the reward for believing; but being thrust out from being one of Christ's disciples, after a visible admission as such, is properly a punishment of unbelief. John 3:18–19: "He that believeth on Him is not condemned; but he that believeth not is condemned already, because he hath not believed in the name of the only begotten Son of God. And this is the condemnation, that light is come into the world, and men loved darkness rather than light, because their deeds were evil."

Salvation is promised to faith as a free gift, but damnation is threatened to unbelief as a debt or punishment due to unbelief. They who believed while in the wilderness did not enter into Canaan because of the worthiness of their faith; but God swore in His wrath that they who believed not should not enter in because of the unworthiness of their unbelief. Admitting a soul to a union with Christ is an act of free and sovereign grace; but excluding at death, and at the day of judgment, those professors of Christianity who have had the offers of a Savior, and enjoyed great privileges as God's people, is a judicial proceeding, and a just punishment of their unworthy treatment of Christ. The design of this saying of Christ's is to make them sensible of the unworthiness of their treatment of Christ who professed Him to be their Lord and Savior, and set Him below father and mother. It is not meant to show the worthiness of loving Him above father and mother.

If a beggar should be offered any great and precious gift, but (as soon as it is offered) should trample it under his feet, it might show him to be unworthy to have it. Or if a malefactor should have his pardon offered him, so that he might be freed from execution, and should only scoff at it, his pardon might be refused him since he is unworthy of it—even though, if he had received it, he would not have had it for his worthiness, or as being recommended to it by his virtue. For his being a malefactor supposes him to be unworthy, and its being offered him to have it only on accepting supposes that the king looks for no worthiness, nothing in him for which he should bestow pardon as a reward. This may teach us how to understand Acts 13:46: "It was necessary that the Word of God should first have been spoken unto you; but seeing ye put it from you, and judge yourselves unworthy of everlasting life, lo, we turn to the Gentiles."

OBJECTION 5. It is objected against the doctrine of justification by faith alone that repentance is evidently spoken of in Scripture as that which is in a special manner the condition of remission of sins; but remission of sins is by all allowed to be that wherein justification (at least) in great part consists.

But it must certainly arise from a misunderstanding of what the Scripture says about repentance to suppose that faith and repentance are two distinct things which in like manner are the conditions of justification. For it is most plain from the Scripture that the condition of justification, or that in us by which we are justified, is but one, and that is faith. Faith and repentance are not two distinct conditions of justification, nor are they two distinct things that together make one condition of justification; but faith comprehends the whole of that

by which we arc justificd, or by which wc come to have
an interest in Christ, and nothing else has a parallel
concern with it in the affair of our salvation. The divines on the other side of this issue themselves are sensible of this, and therefore they suppose that the faith
the Apostle Paul speaks of, which he says we are justified by alone, comprehends in it repentance.

And therefore, in answer to the objection, I would
say that when repentance is spoken of in Scripture as
the condition of pardon, thereby is not intended any
particular grace or act properly distinct from faith that
has a parallel influence with it in the affair of our pardon or justification; but by repentance is intended
nothing distinct from active conversion (or conversion
actively considered) as it respects the term from which
it comes. Active conversion is a motion or exercise of
the mind that respects two terms, sin and God; and by
repentance is meant this conversion, or active change
of the mind, so far as it is conversant about the term
from which it comes, or about sin. This is what the
word "repentance" properly signifies; in the original of
the New Testament it is *metanoia,* and signifies a change
of the mind, or, which is the same thing, the turning
or the conversion of the mind. Repentance is this turning, as it respects that which is turned from. Acts 26:19–
20: "Whereupon, O king Agrippa, I showed unto them
of Damascus, and at Jerusalem, and throughout all the
coasts of Judea, and then to the Gentiles, that they
should repent and turn to God." Both of these concepts
in the last phrase are the same turning, but only with
respect to opposite terms. In the former is expressed
the exercise of mind about sin in this turning; in the
other, the exercise of mind towards God.

If we look over the scriptures that speak of evangelical repentance, we shall immediately see that repentance is to be understood in this sense. Matthew 9:13: "I am not come to call the righteous, but sinners to repentance." Luke 13:3: "Except ye repent, ye shall all likewise perish." Luke 15:7, 10: "There is joy in heaven over one sinner that repenteth," that is, over one sinner who is converted. Acts 11:18: "Then hath God also to the Gentiles granted repentance unto life." This is said by the Christians of the circumcised persons at Jerusalem upon Peter's giving an account of the conversion of Cornelius and his family, and their embracing the gospel, though Peter had said nothing expressly about their sorrow for sin. Acts 17:30: "But now God commandeth all men everywhere to repent." Luke 16:30: "Nay, father Abraham, but if one went to them from the dead, they would repent." 2 Peter 3:9: "The Lord is not slack concerning His promise, as some men count slackness, but is longsuffering to usward, not willing that any should perish, but that all should come to repentance." It is plain that in these and other places, "repentance" means "conversion."

Now it is true that conversion is the condition of pardon and justification; but, if it is so, how absurd is it to say that conversion is one condition of justification and faith another, as though they were two distinct and parallel conditions! Conversion is the condition of justification because it is that great change by which we are brought from sin to Christ, and by which we become believers in Him. This is agreeable to Matthew 21:32: "And ye, when ye had seen it, repented not afterward, that ye might believe Him." When we are directed to repent that our sins may be blotted out, it is as much

as to say, "Let your minds and hearts be changed that
your sins may be blotted out." But if it be said, "Let your
hearts be changed so that you may be justified, and believe that you may be justified," does it therefore follow
that the changed heart is one condition of justification
and believing another? But our minds must be
changed so that we may believe, and so may be justified.

Besides, evangelical repentance, being active conversion, is not to be treated as a particular grace properly and entirely distinct from faith, as by some it seems
to have been. What is conversion but the sinful, alienated soul's closing with Christ, or the sinner's being
brought to believe in Christ? That exercise of soul in
conversion that respects sin cannot be excluded out of
the nature of faith in Christ; there is something in
faith, or closing with Christ, that respects sin, and that
is evangelical repentance. That repentance which in
Scripture is called "repentance for the remission of
sins" is that very principle or operation of the mind itself that is called faith, so far as it is conversant about
sin.

Justifying faith in a Mediator is conversant about
two things: it is conversant about sin or evil to be rejected and to be delivered from, and about positive
good to be accepted and obtained through the Mediator. As for the former of these, it constitutes evangelical
repentance, or repentance for the remission of sins.
Surely they must be very ignorant, or at least very
inconsiderate, of the whole tenor of the gospel who
think that the repentance by which remission of sin is
obtained can be completed, as to all that is essential to
it, without any respect to Christ or application of the
mind to the Mediator, who alone has made atonement

for sin. Surely so great a part of salvation as remission
of sins is not to be obtained without looking or coming
to the great and only Savior. It is true that repentance,
in its more general, abstract nature, is only a sorrow for
sin and forsaking of it, which is a duty of natural religion; but evangelical repentance, or repentance for the
remission of sins, has more than this as essential to it.
A dependence of the soul on the Mediator for deliverance from sin is of the essence of it.

That justifying repentance has the nature of faith
seems evident by Acts 19:4: "Then said Paul, 'John verily
baptized with the baptism of repentance, saying unto
the people that they should believe on Him which
should come after him, that is, on Christ Jesus.' " The
latter words, "saying unto the people that they should
believe on Him," are evidently exegetical of the former,
and explain how he preached repentance for the remission of sin. When it is said that he preached repentance for the remission of sin, saying that they should
believe on Christ, it cannot be supposed but that his
saying that they should believe on Christ was intended
as directing them what to do that they might obtain the
remission of sins. So 2 Timothy 2:25: "In meekness in-
structing those that oppose themselves, if God peradventure will give them repentance to the acknowledging of the truth." That acknowledging of the truth
which which is part of believing is here spoken of as
what is attained in repentance. And on the other hand,
that faith includes repentance in its nature is evident
by the apostle's speaking of sin as destroyed in faith
(Galatians 2:18). In the preceding verses the apostle
mentions an objection against the doctrine of justification by faith alone, which is that it tends to encourage

men in sin, and so to make Christ the minister of sin. This objection he rejects and refutes with this: "If I build again the things that I destroyed, I make myself a transgressor." If sin is destroyed by faith, it must be by repentance of sin included in it; for we know that it is our repentance of sin, or our *metanoia,* or turning of the mind from sin, that is our destroying our sin.

That part of justifying faith which directly respects sin, or the evil to be delivered from by the Mediator, is as follows: a sense of our own sinfulness, our hatred of it, and a hearty acknowledgment of its deserving the threatened punishment, combined with looking to the free mercy of God in a Redeemer for deliverance from it and its punishment.

Concerning this point here described, three things may be noted as explained in the paragraphs that follow: (1) it is the very same as that evangelical repentance to which remission of sins is promised in Scripture; (2) it is of the essence of justifying faith, and is the same as that faith, so far as it is conversant about evil to be delivered from by the Mediator; and (3) this is indeed the proper and peculiar condition of remission of sins.

1. All of this is essential to evangelical repentance, and is indeed the very thing meant by that repentance to which remission of sins is promised in the gospel. As to the former part of the description—that it is a sense of our own sinfulness, our hatred of it, and a hearty acknowledgment of its deserving wrath—none will deny that it is included in repentance; but this does not comprehend the whole essence of evangelical repentance. What also properly and essentially belongs to its nature is our looking to the free mercy of God in a Redeemer for deliverance from it and its punishment. That repentance to which remission is promised not only always has this with it, but it is contained in it as what is of the proper nature and essence of it; and respect is ever had to this in the nature of repentance whenever remission is promised to it. It is especially out of respect to this part of the nature of repentance that it has that promise made to it. If this latter part is missing, it fails to be of the nature of that evangelical repentance to which remission of sins is promised. If repentance remains in sorrow for sin, and does not include looking to the free mercy of God in Christ for pardon, it is not that which is the condition of pardon; neither shall pardon be obtained by it.

Evangelical repentance is a humiliation for sin before God; but the sinner never comes and humbles himself before God in any other repentance but that which includes hopes in his mercy for remission. If sorrow is not accompanied with that, there will be no coming to God in it, but a flying further from Him. There is some worship of God in justifying repentance, but it is not in any other repentance which has no sense of and faith in the divine mercy to forgive sin. Psalm 130:4: "There is forgiveness with Thee, that Thou mayest be feared." The promise of mercy to a true penitent in Proverbs 28:13 is expressed in these terms: "Whoso confesseth and forsaketh his sins shall have mercy." But there is faith in God's mercy in that confession. The psalmist (Psalm 32) speaks of the blessedness of the man whose transgression is forgiven, and whose sin is covered, to whom the Lord imputes not sin. He says that while he kept silence his bones waxed old; but he acknowledged his sin unto God, and his iniquity he did not hide. He said that he would confess his transgression to the Lord, and then God forgave the iniquity of his sin.

The manner of expression plainly holds forth that then he began to encourage himself in the mercy of God, but his bones waxed old while he kept silence. And therefore the Apostle Paul, in Romans 4, brings this example to confirm the doctrine of justification by faith alone that he had been insisting on. When sin is rightly confessed to God, there is always faith in that act. That confession of sin which is joined with despair, as in the case of Judas, is not the confession to which the promise is made. In Acts 2:38, the direction given to those who were pricked in their heart with a sense of the guilt of sin was to repent and be baptized in the name of Jesus Christ for the remission of their sins. Being baptized in the name of Christ for the remission of sins implied faith in Christ for the remission of sins. Repentance for the remission of sins was typified of old by the priest's confessing the sins of the people over the scapegoat, laying his hands on him (Leviticus 16:21), denoting that only that repentance and confession of sin obtain remission which are made over Christ the great sacrifice, and with dependence on Him. Many other things might be produced from the Scripture that in like manner confirm this point, but these may be sufficient.

2. All the aforementioned description is of the essence of justifying faith, and not different from it, so far as it is conversant about sin, or the evil to be delivered from by the Mediator. For it is doubtless of the essence of justifying faith to embrace Christ as a Savior from sin and its punishment, and all that is contained in that act is contained in the nature of faith itself. But in the act of embracing Christ as a

Savior from our sin and its punishment is implied a sense of our sinfulness and a hatred of our sins, or a rejecting them with abhorrence, and a sense of our deserving punishment. Embracing Christ as a Savior from sin implies the contrary act, that is, rejecting sin. If we fly to the light to be delivered from darkness, the same act is contrary to darkness, that is, rejecting it. In proportion to the earnestness with which we embrace Christ as a Savior from sin is the abhorrence with which we reject sin in the same act.

Suppose that there is, in the nature of faith as conversant about sin, no more than the hearty embracing of Christ as a Savior from the punishment of sin; this act will imply in it the whole of the above-mentioned description. It implies a sense of our own sinfulness. Certainly in the hearty embracing of a Savior from the punishment of our sinfulness there is the exercise of a sense that we are sinful. We cannot heartily embrace Christ as a Savior from the punishment of that which we are not sensible that we are guilty of. There is also in the same act a sense of our deserving the threatened punishment. We cannot heartily embrace Christ as a Savior from that which we are not sensible that we have deserved. For if we are not sensible that we have deserved the punishment, we shall not be sensible that we have any need of a Savior from it, or, at least, shall not be convinced that God, who offers the Savior, does not unjustly makes Him needful; and we cannot heartily embrace such an offer.

Further, there is implied in heartily embracing Christ as a Savior from punishment not only a conviction of conscience, that we have deserved the punishment as the devils and damned have, but also a hearty acknowledgment of this, with the submission of the soul, so as, with the accord of the heart, to agree that God might be just in the punishment. If the heart rises against the act or judgment of God in holding us obliged to the punishment, when he offers us His Son as a Savior from the punishment, we cannot with the consent of the heart receive Him for that purpose. But if persons thus submit to the righteousness of so dreadful a punishment of sin, this carries in it a hatred of sin.

That such a sense of our sinfulness, utter unworthiness, and deserving punishment belongs to the nature of saving faith is what the Scripture from time to time holds forth, as particularly in Matthew 15:26–28: "But He answered and said, 'It is not meet to take the children's bread, and to cast it to dogs.' And she said, 'Truth, Lord; yet the dogs eat of the crumbs which fall from their masters' table.' Then Jesus answered and said unto her, 'O woman, great is thy faith.' " And Luke 7:6–9: "The centurion sent friends to Him, saying unto Him, 'Lord, trouble not Thyself, for I am not worthy that Thou shouldest enter under my roof. Wherefore neither thought I myself worthy to come unto Thee; but say in a word, and my servant shall be healed. For I also am a man set under authority.' When Jesus heard these things, He marveled at him, and turned him about, and said unto the people that followed Him, 'I say unto you, I have not found so great faith, no, not in Israel.' " And verses 37–38: "And behold, a woman in the city, which was a sinner, when she knew that Jesus sat at meat in the Pharisee's house, brought an alabaster box of ointment, and stood at His feet behind Him weeping, and began to wash His feet with tears, and did wipe them with the hairs of her head, and kissed His feet, and anointed them with the ointment." Then verse 50: "He said to the woman, 'Thy faith hath saved thee; go in peace.' "

These things do not necessarily suppose that repentance and faith are words of just the same significance; for it is only that part of justifying faith that respects the evil to be delivered from by the Savior that is called repentance. Besides, both repentance, and faith, taken only in their general nature, are entirely distinct: repentance is a sorrow for sin and a forsaking of it, and faith is trusting in God's sufficiency and truth. But faith and repentance, as evangelical duties, or justifying faith and repentance for the remission of sins, contain more in them, and imply a respect to a Mediator, and involve each other's nature, though they still bear the name of faith and repentance from those general moral virtues—that repentance which is a duty of natural religion, and that faith which was a duty required under the first covenant—that are contained in this evangelical act. The distinctives appear when this act is considered with respect to its different terms and objects.

It may be objected here that the Scripture sometimes mentions faith and repentance together as if they were entirely distinct things. Mark 1:15: "Repent ye, and believe the gospel." But there is no need of understanding these as two distinct conditions of salvation; the words are exegetical of one another. It is to teach us after what manner we must repent (believing the gospel), and after what manner we must believe the gospel (repenting). These words no more prove faith and repentance to be entirely distinct than those aforementioned

in Matthew 21:32: "And ye, when ye had seen it, repented not afterwards, that ye might believe him"; or
those in 2 Timothy 2:25: "If peradventure God will give
them repentance to the acknowledging of the truth."
In Acts 19:4, the apostle seems to have reference to
these words of John the Baptist: "John baptized with the
baptism of repentance, saying unto the people that they
should believe"; the latter phrase, as we have already
observed, explains how he preached repentance.

Another Scripture where faith and repentance are
mentioned together is Acts 20:21: "Testifying, both to
the Jews and also to the Greeks, repentance toward God
and faith toward our Lord Jesus Christ." It may be objected that, in this place, faith and repentance are not
only spoken of as distinct things, but as having distinct
objects.

To this I answer that faith and repentance, in their
general nature, are distinct things; and repentance for
the remission of sins, or that part of justifying faith that
respects the evil to be delivered from, so far as it regards
our sin (which is what especially denominates it repentance), has respect to God as the object, because He is
the Being offended by sin and to be reconciled. But
that part of this justifying act which is denominated
"faith" more especially respects Christ. But interpret it
how we will, the objection of faith being here so distinguished from repentance is as much of an objection
against the scheme of those who oppose justification by
faith alone as against this scheme; for they hold that
the justifying faith the Apostle Paul speaks of includes
repentance, as has been already observed.

*3. This repentance that has been described is indeed the special
condition of remission of sins.* This seems very evident by the

Scripture, particularly Mark 1:4: "John did baptize in the wilderness, and preach the baptism of repentance for the remission of sins." So Luke 3:3: "And he came into all the country about Jordan, preaching the baptism of repentance, for the remission of sins." Luke 24:47: "And that repentance and remission of sins should be preached in His name among all nations." Acts 5:31: "Him hath God exalted with His right hand to be a Prince and a Savior, to give repentance unto Israel, and forgiveness of sins." Acts 2:38. "Repent, and be baptized every one of you in the name of Jesus Christ for the remission of sins." And Acts 3:19: "Repent ye therefore, and be converted, that your sins may be blotted out." The like is evident by Leviticus 26:40–42; Job 33:27–28; Psalm 32:5; Proverbs 28:13; Jeremiah 3:13; 1 John 1:9; and other places.

The reason may be plain from what has been said. We need not wonder that what in faith especially respects sin would be especially the condition of remission of sins, or that this motion or exercise of the soul—as it rejects and flies from evil, and embraces Christ as a Savior from it—should especially be the condition of being free from that evil. Rather, it is natural that the same principle or motion, as it seeks good and cleaves to Christ as the procurer of that good, should also be the condition of obtaining that good. Faith accepts good and rejects evil, and this rejecting of evil is itself an act of acceptance; it is accepting freedom or separation from that evil, and this freedom or separation is the benefit bestowed in remission of sin. No wonder that the part of faith that immediately respects this benefit, and is our acceptance of it, should be the special condition of our having it. It is so with respect to all the benefits that Christ has purchased. Trusting in God through Christ for such a particular benefit that we need is always the special condition of obtaining that benefit. When we need protection from enemies, the exercise of faith with respect to such a benefit, or trusting in Christ for protection from enemies, is especially the way to obtain that particular benefit, rather than trusting in Christ for something else— and so of any other benefit that might be mentioned. So prayer (which is the expression of faith) for a particular mercy needed is especially the way to obtain that mercy.

So no argument can be drawn from hence against the doctrine of justification by faith alone. And there is that in the nature of repentance which peculiarly tends to establish the opposite of justification by works, for nothing so much renounces our own worthiness and excellence as repentance; the very nature of it is to acknowledge our own utter sinfulness and unworthiness, and to renounce our own goodness and all confidence in oneself, and so to trust in the propitiation of the Mediator and ascribe all the glory of forgiveness to Him.

OBJECTION 6. The last objection I shall mention is that paragraph in James 2, where persons are said expressly to be justified by works. James 2:21: "Was not Abraham our father justified by works?" Verse 24: "Ye see then that by works a man is justified, and not by faith only." Verse 25: "Was not Rahab the harlot justified by works?"

In answer to this objection, I would:

1. Take notice of the great unfairness of the divines

who oppose us in the application they make of this passage against us. All will allow that in St. James's proposition, "By works a man is justified, and not by faith only," one of the terms, either the word "faith" or the word "justify," is not to be understood precisely in the same sense as the same terms when used by St. Paul. That is because they suppose, as well as we, that it was not the intent of the Apostle James to contradict St. Paul in that doctrine of justification by faith alone in which he had instructed the churches. But if we understand both terms, as used by each apostle, in precisely the same sense, then what one asserts is a precise, direct, and full contradiction of the other, the one affirming and the other denying the very same thing.

So that all the controversy from this text comes to which of these two terms shall be understood differently from St. Paul. They say that it is the word "faith," for they suppose that when the Apostle Paul uses the word, and makes faith that by which alone we are justified, that by it we are to understand a compliance with and practice of Christianity in general, so as to include all saving Christian virtue and obedience. But as the Apostle James uses the word "faith" in this passage, they suppose that he means only an assent of the understanding to the truth of gospel doctrines as distinguished from good works, and that this assent may exist separate from such works, and from all saving grace.

We, on the other hand, suppose that the word "justify" is to be understood in a different sense from the Apostle Paul. So they are forced to go as far in their scheme in altering the sense of terms from Paul's use of them as we. But at the same time that they freely vary the sense of "faith," yet when we understand "justify" in

a different sense from St. Paul, they cry out against us.
"What necessity is there of framing this distinction but
only to serve an opinion?" they declare. "At this rate a
man may maintain anything, though never so contrary
to Scripture, and elude the clearest text in the Bible!"
But they do not show us why we do not have as good a
warrant to understand the word "justify" differently
from St. Paul as they do for the word "faith." If the sense
of one of the words must be varied on either scheme to
make the Apostle James's doctrine consistent with the
Apostle Paul's; and if varying the sense of one term or
the other is all that stands in the way of their agreeing
with either scheme; and if varying the sense of the latter is in itself as fair as of the former—then the text lies
as fair for one scheme as the other, and can no more
fairly be an objection against our scheme than theirs.
And, if so, what becomes of all this great objection
from this passage in James?

2. If there is no more difficulty in varying the sense
of one of these terms than another from anything in
the text itself, so as to make the words suit with either
scheme, then certainly the same is true of Scripture,
and other places where the same matter is more particularly and fully treated; and therefore we should understand the word "justify" in the James passage in a sense
in some respect different from that in which St. Paul
uses it. For by what has been already said, it may appear
that there is no one doctrine in the whole Bible more
fully asserted, explained, and urged than the doctrine
of justification by faith alone, without any of our own
righteousness.

3. There is a very fair interpretation of the James passage which shows that it is in no way inconsistent with

this doctrine of justification. I have shown that other scriptures abundantly teach this, and the words of James themselves will as well allow this interpretation as that which the objectors put upon them, and it much better agrees with the context. It is that works are here spoken of as justifying as evidences. A man may be said to be justified by that which clears or vindicates him, or makes the goodness of his cause manifest.

When a person has a case tried in a civil court, and is justified or cleared, he may be said in different senses to be justified or cleared by the goodness of his case, and by the goodness of the evidences of it. He may be said to be cleared by what evidences his case to be good, but not in the same sense as he is by that which makes his case good. That which renders his case good is the proper ground of his justification; it is by that that he is himself a proper subject of it. But evidences justify only as they manifest that his case is good in fact, whether they are of such a nature as to have any influence to render it so or not.

It is by works that our case appears to be good; but by faith our case not only appears to be good, but becomes good, because thereby we are united to Christ. That the word "justify" should be sometimes understood to signify the former of these as well as the latter is agreeable to the use of the word in common speech. We say that such a one stood up to justify another, meaning that he endeavored to show or manifest his case to be good. And it is certain that the word is sometimes used in this sense in Scripture when it speaks of our being justified before God. Matthew 12:37 says that we shall be justified by our words: "For by thy words thou shalt be justified, and by thy words thou shalt be

condemned." It cannot mean that men are accepted before God on the account of their words; for God has
told us nothing more plainly than that it is the heart
that He looks at, and that when He acts as Judge towards men, in order to justify or condemn them, He
tries the heart. Jeremiah 11:20: "But, O Lord of hosts,
that judgest righteously, that triest the reins and the
heart, let me see Thy vengeance on them; for unto
Thee have I revealed my cause." Psalm 7:8–9: "The Lord
shall judge the people: judge me, O Lord, according to
my righteousness, and according to mine integrity that
is in me. Oh, let the wickedness of the wicked come to
an end, but establish the just; for the righteous God tri-
eth the hearts and reins." Verse 11: "God judgeth the
righteous." There are many other places to the same
purpose. And therefore men can be justified by their
words in no other way than as evidences or manifesta-
tions of what is in the heart. It is thus that Christ speaks
of the words in this very passage, as is evident by the
context of Matthew 12:34–35: "Out of the abundance of
the heart the mouth speaketh. A good man out of the
good treasure of the heart bringeth forth good things."
The words, or sounds themselves, are neither parts of
godliness nor evidences of godliness, but signs of what
is inward.

God Himself, when He acts towards men as Judge,
in order to reach a declarative judgment, makes use of
evidences, and so judges men by their works. And therefore, at the day of judgment, God will judge men according to their works; for though God will stand in no
need of evidence to inform Him of what is right, yet it
is to be considered that He will then sit in judgment
not as earthly judges do, to find out what is right in a

case, but to declare and manifest what is right. And therefore that day is called by the apostle "the day of revelation of the righteous judgment of God" (Romans 2:5).

To be justified is to be approved of and accepted. But a man may be said to be approved and accepted in two respects: the one is to be approved really, and the other is to be approved and accepted declaratively. Justification is twofold: it is either the acceptance and approbation of the judge itself, or the manifestation of that approbation by a sentence or judgment declared by the judge, either to our own consciences or to the world. If justification is understood in the former sense, for the approbation itself, it is only that by which we become fit to be approved; but if it is understood in the latter sense, for the manifestation of this approbation, it is by whatever is a proper evidence of that fitness. In the former, only faith is concerned, because it is by that only in us that we become fit to be accepted and approved; in the latter, whatever is an evidence of our fitness is similarly concerned. And therefore, if we take justification in this sense, then faith, and all other graces and good works, have a common and equal concern in it: for any other grace or holy act is equally an evidence of a qualification for acceptance or approbation as is faith.

To justify has always, in common speech, signified interchangeably either simply approbation or testifying to that approbation—sometimes one and sometimes the other, because they are both the same, except that one is outwardly what the other is inwardly. So we and, it may be, all nations are wont to give the same name to two things when one is only declarative of the other.

Thus, sometimes, judging means only judging in our thoughts; at other times, it means testifying and declaring judgment. So such words as "justify," "condemn," "accept," "reject," "prize," "slight," "approve," and "renounce" are sometimes put for mental acts, and at other times for an outward treatment. So, in the sense in which the Apostle James seems to use the word "justify" for manifested justification, a man is justified not only by faith, but also by works, just as a tree is manifested to be good not only by immediately examining the tree, but also by the fruit. Proverbs 20:11: "Even as a child is known by his doing, whether his work be pure, and whether it be right."

The drift of the apostle does not require that he should be understood in any other sense; for all that he aims at, as appears by a view of the context, is to prove that good works are necessary. The error of those whom he opposed was this: good works were not necessary to salvation, but if people simply believed that there was but one God, and that Christ was the Son of God, and the like, and were baptized, they were safe, let them live how they would. And this doctrine greatly tended to licentiousness. To evince the contrary of this is evidently the apostle's scope.

And that we should understand the apostle to be speaking of works justifying as an evidence, as in a declarative judgment, is what a due consideration of the context will naturally lead us to. For it is plain that the apostle is here insisting on works in the quality of a necessary manifestation and evidence of faith, or as what the truth of faith is made to appear by. James 2:18: "Show me thy faith without thy works, and I will show thee my faith by my works." When he says in verse 26,

"As the body without the spirit is dead, so faith without works is dead also," it is much more rational and natural to understand him as speaking of works as the proper signs and evidences of the reality, life, and goodness of faith. Not that the very works or actions done are properly the life of faith, as the spirit in the body, but it is the active, working nature of faith, of which the actions or works done are the signs, that is itself the life and spirit of faith.

The sign of a thing is often in Scripture language said to be that thing, as it is in that comparison by which the apostle illustrates it. Not the actions themselves of a body are properly the life or spirit of the body, but the active nature of which those actions or motions are the signs is the life of the body. That which makes men pronounce anything to be alive is that they observe that it has an active operative nature, which they observe only by the actions or motions which are the signs of it. Plainly, the apostle's aim is to prove that if faith does not have works, it is a sign that it is not a good sort of faith. This would not have been to his purpose if his design had been to show that it is not by faith alone—though of a right sort—that we have acceptance with God, but that we are accepted on account of our obedience as well as faith. It is evident by the apostle's reasoning that the necessity of works is not from their having a parallel concern in our salvation with faith; rather, he speaks of works only as related to faith and expressive of it, which leaves faith as the only fundamental condition, without anything else having a parallel concern with it in this affair. Other things are conditions only as various expressions and evidences of faith.

That the apostle speaks of works as justifying only as a sign or evidence, and in God's declarative judgment, is further confirmed by verse 21: "Was not Abraham our father justified by works, when he had offered up Isaac his son upon the altar?" Here the apostle seems plainly to refer to that declarative judgment of God concerning Abraham's sincerity, manifested to him for the peace and assurance of his own conscience after he offered up Isaac his son on the altar. Genesis 22:12: "Now I know that thou fearest God, seeing thou hast not withheld thy son, thine only son, from Me." But here it is plain, and expressed in the very words of justification or approbation, that this work of Abraham in offering up his son on the altar justified him as an evidence. When the Apostle James says that we are justified by works, he may and ought to be understood in a sense agreeable to the example he brings to prove it; but justification in that example appears, by the words of justification themselves, to be by works as an evidence. And where this instance of Abraham's obedience is elsewhere mentioned in the New Testament it is mentioned as a fruit and evidence of his faith. Hebrews 11:17: "By faith Abraham, when he was tried, offered up Isaac; and he that had received the promises offered up his only begotten son."

The other instance which the apostle mentions is in verse 25: "Likewise also was not Rahab the harlot justified by works, when she had received the messengers, and had sent them out another way?" The apostle refers to a declarative judgment, in that particular testimony which was given of God's approbation of her as a believer, in directing Joshua to save her when the rest of Jericho was destroyed. Joshua 6:25: "And Joshua saved

Rahab the harlot alive, and her father's household, and all that she had, and she dwelleth in Israel even unto this day, because she hid the messengers which Joshua sent to spy out Jericho." This was accepted as an evidence and expression of her faith. Hebrews 11:31: "By faith the harlot Rahab perished not with them that believed not, when she had received the spies with peace." The apostle, in saying, "Was not Rahab the harlot justified by works?" by the manner of his speaking has reference to something in her history; but we have no account in her history of any other justification of her but this.

4. If, notwithstanding, any choose to take justification in St. James's precisely as we do in Paul's epistles, for God's acceptance or approbation itself, and not any expression of that approbation, what has been already said concerning the manner in which acts of evangelical obedience are concerned in the affair of our justification affords a very easy, clear, and full answer. For if we take works as acts or expressions of faith, they are not excluded; so a man is not justified by faith only, but also by works—that is, he is not justified only by faith as a principle in the heart, or in its first and more immanent acts, but also by the effective acts of it in life, which are the expressions of the life of faith, as the operations and actions of the body are of the life of the body. All this is agreeable to James 2:26.

What has been said in answer to these objections may also, I hope, abundantly serve as an answer to another objection which is often made against this doctrine: that it encourages licentiousness in life. For, from what has been said, we may see that the Scripture doctrine of justification by faith alone, without any

manner of goodness or excellence of ours, in no way
diminishes either the necessity or benefit of a sincere,
evangelical, universal obedience. Man's salvation is not
only indissolubly connected with obedience, and
damnation with the want of it, in those who have opportunity for it, but depends upon it in many respects.
It is the way to salvation, and the necessary preparation
for it; eternal blessings are bestowed in reward for it,
and our justification in our own consciences and at the
day of judgment depends on it as the proper evidence
of our acceptable state, and that even in accepting us as
entitled to life in our justification.

God has respect to this obedience as that on which
the fitness of such an act of justification depends, so
that our salvation as truly depends upon it as if we were
justified for the moral excellence of it. And besides all
this, the degree of our happiness to all eternity is suspended on and determined by the degree of our obedience. So this gospel-scheme of justification is as far
from encouraging licentiousness, and contains as
much to encourage and excite to strict and universal
obedience, and the utmost possible eminence of holiness, as any scheme that can be devised, and, indeed,
unspeakably more.

Chapter 6

The Importance of the Doctrine

I know there are many who think this controversy is of no great importance, and that it is chiefly a matter of nice speculation, depending on certain subtle distinctions, which many who make use of them do not understand themselves. They believe the difference is not of such consequence as to be worth being zealous about, and that more harm is done by raising disputes about it than good.

Indeed, I am far from thinking that it is of absolute necessity that persons should understand and be agreed upon all the distinctions needful to explain and defend this doctrine against all cavils and objections. Yet all Christians should strive after an increase of knowledge, and none should content themselves without some clear and distinct understanding in this point. But we should believe in general, according to the clear and abundant revelations of God's Word, that it is none of our own excellence, virtue, or righteousness that is the ground of our being received from a state of condemnation into a state of acceptance in God's sight, but only Jesus Christ and His righteousness and worthiness received by faith. This I think to be of great importance, at least in application to ourselves, and that for the following reasons:

1. The Scripture treats this doctrine as a doctrine of very great importance. That there is a certain doctrine of justification by faith, in opposition to justification by

the works of the law, which the Apostle Paul insists
upon as of the greatest importance, none will deny, because there is nothing in the Bible more apparent. The
apostle, under the infallible conduct of the Spirit of
God, thought it worth his most strenuous and zealous
disputation and defense. He speaks of the contrary doctrine as fatal and ruinous to the souls of men, in the
latter verses of Romans 9 and the beginning of Romans
10. He speaks of it as subversive of the gospel of Christ,
calls it "another gospel," and says, concerning it, that if
anyone, "though an angel from heaven, preach it, let
him be accursed" (Galatians 1:6–9). Certainly we must
allow the apostles, when the Spirit is speaking through
them, to be good judges of the importance and tendency of doctrines. And doubtless we are safe, and in
no danger of harshness and censoriousness, if we only
follow him and keep close to his express teachings in
what we believe and say of the hurtful and pernicious
tendency of any error. Why are we to blame for saying
what the Bible has taught us to say, or for believing
what the Holy Ghost has taught us to the end that we
might believe it?

2. The adverse scheme lays another foundation of
man's salvation than God has laid. I do not now speak
of that ineffectual redemption that they suppose to be
universal, and what all mankind are equally the subjects of; but, I say, it lays entirely another foundation of
man's actual, discriminating salvation, or that salvation wherein true Christians differ from wicked men.
We suppose the foundation of this to be Christ's worthiness and righteousness; on the contrary, that
scheme supposes it to be men's own virtue, and even
proposes that this is the ground of a saving interest in

Christ itself. It takes Christ out of the place of the bottom stone, and puts men's own virtue in place of Him. So that Christ Himself, in the affair of distinguishing actual salvation, is laid upon this foundation. And that foundation being so different, I leave it to everyone to judge whether the difference between the two schemes consists only in punctilios of small consequence. The foundation, being contrary, makes the whole scheme exceedingly diverse and opposite: the one is a gospel scheme, the other a legal one.

3. It is in this doctrine that the most essential difference lies between the covenant of grace and the first covenant. The adverse scheme of justification supposes that we are justified by our works in the very same sense wherein man was to have been justified by his works under the first covenant. By that covenant our first parents were not to have had eternal life given them for any proper merit in their obedience, because their perfect obedience was a debt that they owed God. Nor was it to be bestowed for any proportion between the dignity of their obedience and the value of the reward, but it was only to be bestowed from a regard for a moral fitness, in the virtue of their obedience, to the reward of God's favor; and a title to eternal life was to be given them as a testimony of God's being pleased with their works, or His regard for the inherent beauty of their virtue. And so it is in the very same way that those in the adverse scheme suppose that we are received into God's special favor now, and to those saving benefits that are the testimonies of it.

I am sensible that the divines who take that side entirely disclaim the popish doctrine of merit, and are free to speak of our utter unworthiness and the great

imperfection of all our services. But, after all, it is our
virtue, imperfect as it is, that recommends men to God,
by which good men come to have a saving interest in
Christ and God's favor, rather than others; and these
things are bestowed in testimony of God's respect for
their goodness. So that, whether they allow the term
"merit" or not, yet they hold that we are accepted by our
own merit in the same sense, though not in the same
degree, as under the first covenant.

But the great and most distinguishing difference
between that covenant and the covenant of grace is
that, by the covenant of grace, we are not thus justified
by our own works, but only by faith in Jesus Christ. It is
on this account chiefly that the new covenant deserves
the name of a covenant of grace, as is evident by
Romans 4:16: "Therefore it is of faith, that it might be
by grace." And Romans 3:20, 24: "Therefore by the deeds
of the law there shall no flesh be justified in His
sight . . . being justified freely by His grace through the
redemption that is in Jesus Christ." And Romans 11:6:
"And if by grace, then it is no more of works; otherwise
grace is no more grace. But if it be of works, then it is
no more grace; otherwise work is no more work."
Galatians 5:4: "Whosoever of you are justified by the law,
ye are fallen from grace." And therefore the apostle, in
the same epistle to the Galatians, speaking of the doctrine of justification by works as another gospel, adds,
"which is not another gospel" (1:6–7). It is no gospel at
all; it is law. It is no covenant of grace, but of works; not
an evangelical, but a legal doctrine. Certainly that doctrine wherein consists the greatest and most essential
difference between the covenant of grace and the first
covenant must be a doctrine of great importance. That

doctrine of the gospel by which, above all others, it is worthy of the name of gospel is doubtless a very important doctrine of the gospel.

4. This is the main thing for which fallen men stood in need of divine revelation, to teach us how we who have sinned may come to be again accepted of God, or, which is the same thing, how the sinner may be justified. Something beyond the light of nature is necessary for salvation chiefly on this account. Mere natural reason afforded no means by which we could come to the knowledge of this, it depending on the sovereign pleasure of the Being whom we had offended by sin. This seems to be the great drift of that revelation which God has given, and of all those mysteries it reveals, all those great doctrines that are peculiarly doctrines of revelation, and above the light of nature. It seems to have been very much on this account that it was necessary that the doctrine of the Trinity itself should be revealed to us, that by a discovery of the concern of the several divine persons in the great affair of our salvation we might better understand and see how all our dependence in this affair is on God, and our sufficiency all in Him and not in ourselves—that He is all in all in this business, as indicated by 1 Corinthians 1:29–31: "That no flesh should glory in His presence. But of Him are ye in Christ Jesus, who of God is made unto us wisdom, and righteousness, and sanctification, and redemption, that, according as it is written, 'He that glorieth, let him glory in the Lord.' " What is the gospel but the glad tidings of a new way of acceptance with God unto life, a way wherein sinners may come to be free from the guilt of sin and obtain a title to eternal life? And if, when this way is revealed, it is rejected, and

another of man's devising is put in its place, without doubt it must be an error of great importance, and the apostle might well say it was "another gospel."

5. The contrary scheme of justification derogates much from the honor of God and the Mediator. I have already shown how it diminishes the glory of the Mediator by ascribing that to man's virtue and goodness which belongs alone to His worthiness and righteousness. As the apostle sees the matter, it renders Christ needless. Galatians 5:4: "Christ is become of no effect to you, whosoever of you are justified by the law." If that scheme of justification is followed in its consequence, it utterly overthrows the glory of all the great things that have been contrived, done, and suffered in the work of redemption. Galatians 2:21: "If righteousness comes by the law, Christ is dead in vain."

It has also been already shown how this scheme diminishes the glory of divine grace (which is the attribute God has especially set Himself to glorify in the work of redemption), and so greatly diminishes the obligation to gratitude in the sinner who is saved. Yea, to quote the apostle again, it makes void the distinguishing grace of the gospel. Galatians 5:4: "Whosoever of you are justified by the law, ye are fallen from grace." It diminishes the glory of the grace of God and the Redeemer, and proportionally magnifies man. It makes the goodness and excellence of fallen man to be something, which I have shown are nothing.

I have also already shown that it is contrary to the truth of God in the threatening of His holy law to justify the sinner for his virtue. And whether it were contrary to God's truth or not, it is a scheme of things very unworthy of God. It supposes that God, when about to lift up a poor, forlorn malefactor condemned to eternal misery for sinning against his Majesty, and to make him unspeakably and eternally happy by bestowing His Son and Himself upon him, as it were, puts all this on sale for the price of his virtue and excellency.

I know that those whom we oppose acknowledge that the price is very disproportionate to the benefit bestowed, and say that God's grace is wonderfully manifested in accepting so little virtue, and bestowing so glorious a reward for such imperfect righteousness. But seeing that we are such infinitely sinful and abominable creatures in God's sight, and by our infinite guilt have brought ourselves into such wretched and deplorable circumstances—and all our righteousness is nothing, and ten thousand times worse than nothing, if God looks upon our actions as they are in themselves—is it not unquestionably more worthy of the infinite majesty and glory of God to deliver and make happy such wretched vagabonds and captives without any money or price of theirs, or any manner of expectation of excellence or virtue in them, in any way to recommend them? Will it not betray a foolish, exalting opinion of ourselves, and a mean one of God, to have thoughts of offering anything of ours to recommend us to the favor of being brought from wallowing like filthy swine in the mire of our sins, and from the enmity and misery of devils in the lowest hell, to the state of God's dear children in the everlasting arms of His love in heavenly glory—or to imagine that it is the constitution of God that we should bring our filthy rags and offer them to Him as the price of this?

6. The opposite scheme most directly tends to lead men to trust in their own righteousness for justifica-

tion, which is a thing fatal to the soul. This is what men are, of themselves, exceedingly prone to do (and that though they are never so much taught the contrary), through the partial and high thoughts they have of themselves, and their exceeding dullness of apprehending any such mystery as our being accepted for the righteousness of another. But this scheme directly teaches men to trust in their own righteousness for justification in that it teaches them that this is indeed what they must be justified by, being the way of justification which God Himself has appointed. So that if a man had naturally no disposition to trust in his own righteousness, yet if he embraced this scheme and acted consistently it would lead him to it. But trusting in our own righteousness is a thing fatal to the soul, as the Scripture plainly teaches us. It tells us that it will cause that Christ shall profit us nothing, and be of no effect to us (Galatians 5:2–4). For though the apostle speaks there particularly of circumcision, yet it is not merely being circumcised, but trusting in circumcision as a means of righteousness, that the apostle has respect to. He could not mean that merely being circumcised would render Christ of no profit or effect to a person; for we read that he himself, for certain reasons, took Timothy and circumcised him (Acts 16:3). And the same is evident by the context, and by the rest of the epistle.

The apostle speaks of trusting in their own righteousness as fatal to the Jews. Romans 9:31–32: "But Israel, which followed after the law of righteousness, hath not attained to the law of righteousness. Wherefore? Because they sought it not by faith, but as it were by the works of the law; for they stumbled at that stumbling-stone." Take this together with Romans 10:3: "For they, being ignorant of God's righteousness, and going about to establish their own righteousness, have not submitted themselves unto the righteousness of God." And this is spoken of as fatal to the Pharisees in the parable of the Pharisee and the publican, which Christ spoke to them in order to reprove them for "trusting in themselves that they were righteous." The design of the parable is to show them that the very publicans shall be justified rather than they, as appears by the reflection Christ makes upon it in Luke 18:14: "I tell you, this man went down to his house justified rather than the other."

The fatal tendency of it might also be proven from its inconsistency with the nature of justifying faith, and with the nature of that humiliation that the Scripture often speaks of as absolutely necessary to salvation. But these scriptures are so express that it is needless to bring any further arguments.

How far a wonderful and mysterious agency of God's Spirit may so influence some men's hearts, that their practice in this regard may be contrary to their own principles, so that they shall not trust in their own righteousness, though they profess that men are justified by their own righteousness; or how far they may believe the doctrine of justification by men's own righteousness in general, and yet not believe it in a particular application of it to themselves; or how far that error which they may have been led into by education, or cunning sophistry of others, may yet be indeed contrary to the prevailing disposition of their hearts, and contrary to their practice; or how far some may seem to maintain a doctrine contrary to this gospel doctrine of justification who really do not, but only express them-

selves differently from others; or how far they may seem
to oppose it through their misunderstanding of our
expressions, or we of theirs, when indeed our real sentiments are the same in the main; or how far they may
seem to differ more than they do by using terms that
are without a precisely fixed and determinate meaning;
or how far they are wide in their sentiments from this
doctrine for want of a distinct understanding of it,
whose hearts, at the same time, entirely agree with it,
and (if once it was clearly explained to their understanding) would immediately close with it and embrace
it—how far these things may be, I will not determine.
But I am fully persuaded that great allowances are to be
made on these and such like accounts in innumerable
instances, though it is manifest from what has been
said that the teaching and propagating of contrary doctrines and schemes is a pernicious and fatal tendency.